Nancy S. Hill

Tyndale House Publishers, Inc.
Wheaton, Illinois

For my sweet inspirations—
Kelsey Vaughan Hill
Stacia Menn Hill
and Maryn Lee Hill—
with all my love.
You'll always be first in my book!

CONTENTS

Why were the police called to an exercise class?

Dr. Hunter was leading an exercise class for a group of elderly patients with arthritis. The senior citizens were supposed to raise their hands over their heads. That was a difficult exercise for them to do, so Dr. Hunter encouraged them by saying loudly, "Stick 'em up!" Just at that moment, someone walking by looked in the window. Soon the members of the exercise class heard sirens. Then police cars surrounded their building. It seems that the person looking in the window thought that he saw a robber holding up the whole class, yelling, "Stick 'em up!" The doctor explained that these oldsters were holding their hands up for their health, not for their safety. Finally the whole misunderstanding was straightened out.

People make mistakes. The person looking through the window thought he knew what was happening, but he didn't. Fortunately, God never makes mistakes. He always knows exactly what's going on. The Bible says, "Lord, you know everyone's heart" (Acts 1:24, NIV). If you're trying to do a good thing, God will know that you wanted to do well, even if it doesn't turn out right. He will understand what you meant to do. Even when you think no one could possibly understand, God does—every time.

2
Which country has a pancake party every year?

Lent is a special time for Christians. It comes in the spring, and people give up certain foods to remind them of when Jesus wandered in the wilderness. Some of the things that are given up are eggs, milk, and fats. Those are exactly the same ingredients that go into pancakes, so in England, people go crazy for pancakes on the day before Lent, using up all the groceries that they won't be needing for a while.

In fact, they have an official Pancake Day, and they celebrate by playing pancake games. One is toss-the-pancake: Someone tosses a pancake up high, and kids jump up to grab it. In another race, women holding frying pans with pancakes in them must run to the finish line while flipping the pancakes up into the air. People say that they run the pancake race to copy a lady who heard the bells announcing the beginning of church and ran to the chapel with a frying pan still in her hand.

England is not the only country where people do strange things with pancakes. In 1984, in Vermont, a giant pancake was made out of two and a half tons of pancake mix. It used 150 pounds of syrup and over 1,000 pounds of butter. It was so big that they needed a helicopter to flip it!

Christians have always set aside time to glorify God, even when it meant making a sacrifice. God doesn't promise that life will be constantly easy if you are a Christian. But he does promise that he will be your strength through everything that happens to you. The Bible says, "In everything we do we try to show that we are true ministers of God. We patiently endure suffering and hardship and trouble of every kind. We have been beaten, put in jail, faced angry mobs, worked to exhaustion, stayed awake through sleepless nights of watching, and gone without food" (2 Corinthians 6:4-5). There will always be troubles on earth because earth isn't heaven, but you can count on God not to leave you to go through your problems alone.

3
Why does a contest usually have first, second, and third place winners?

If you thought it was because the judges were trying to be kind by letting more than one person win, you would be wrong. If you thought more people would enter a contest if there were more prizes, that's not the reason either. The real reason will surprise you.

Long ago, in the 1600s, there was a horse race in England. The sheriff was in charge of the race and the prizes. He asked the silversmith to make a beautiful silver trophy for the winner. The silversmith went to work and returned to the sheriff with the trophy. But the sheriff didn't think it was grand enough for a prize. He told the silversmith to try again and sent him back to his shop. Later, the silversmith brought his second trophy to be inspected. Once again, the sheriff said no, the trophy wasn't quite good enough. The silversmith went back to work. When he was finished making the third trophy, he took it to the sheriff, and this time, it was perfect. You would think the sheriff would be happy, but instead he discovered he had a problem. He had three trophies now, but only one winner. The sheriff didn't want to waste the other two trophies, so he decided to have two more winners.

Many people have gotten prizes because that sheriff was so picky!

Trophies are fun to win, but after time has gone by, they can get old and tarnished and rusty. God has promised us some prizes at the end of our lives, and they will never get old. The Bible tells us, "He will give eternal life to those who patiently do the will of God, seeking for the unseen glory and honor and eternal life that he offers" (Romans 2:7). The trophies of glory and honor and eternal life can't be looked at, held in our hands, or kept on a shelf. But they are the best rewards we could ever win, and they will belong to us forever.

When was a sunny day bad for baseball?

It was a sports fan's dream come true—no more games cancelled because of bad weather. The Astrodome in Houston opened in 1965. It was a huge stadium with clear plastic panels in the roof to let the sun in. Everyone was excited that the dome was finally built, and it wasn't until the first baseball game was played inside that people realized there was a problem. The skylights were letting in so much sunlight that when the players looked up, they kept missing the ball because of the glare. And the steel girders that held up the ceiling crisscrossed so much that the ball seemed to get lost in the air. No one had expected this mistake, and lots of people tried to think of a way to fix it. Maybe the players could use a neon orange ball. Perhaps special sunglasses could be used. The solution that worked was to paint all 4,596 ceiling panels a dark color. Then the glare was gone, and athletes could once again "Play ball!"

The Astrodome is huge, and so was its problem. The owners still found a good solution. When you make a mistake, no matter how big it is, you don't have to figure out a way to fix it. The Bible already tells you what to do. You need to talk to God. The Bible says, "If we confess our sins to him, he can be depended on to forgive us and to cleanse us from every wrong" (1 John 1:9). If you've done something wrong, make it right by going right to God.

———————5

Which fish takes aim at its lunch?

A kind of fish called an *archer* has an interesting way of getting a meal. The archer likes to eat insects. The problem is, most insects are flying above the water's surface. But the archer has a solution. This fish swims to the surface of the water and puts its mouth near the top. Then the archer does something amazing. It spits a stream of water up into the air, and the water hits an insect flying by. The water knocks the insect into the water, and the archer is able to gobble it up.

The archer has a special talent. If you were in charge of giving talents to fish, would you have thought of making a fish that spits water? God's imagination is so much more creative than ours. God has made the world a fascinating place! The Bible says, "God created great sea animals, and every sort of fish and every kind of bird. And God looked at them with pleasure" (Genesis 1:21-22). We have fun looking at God's creatures, too!

6
What did people do about their cuts before Band-Aids?

People helped their cuts to heal by smearing a cream made from the myrrh plant onto a piece of cloth and sticking the cloth to their skin with honey. Fortunately for us, Earl Dickson came up with a better idea in 1920.

Earl's wife was so clumsy that she was forever cutting herself in the kitchen while preparing meals. He usually bandaged her wounds by taping some gauze over the cuts. Earl decided to make some bandages that his wife could put on by herself when he wasn't home. He cut lots of pieces of tape, laid them sticky-side up on a table, and laid a patch of gauze on each one. He covered each bandage to keep the tape from drying out or sticking to itself. Now when Earl's wife got hurt, she could just peel a bandage and stick it on. Earl's boss at Johnson & Johnson liked this new idea and began to sell the bandages, which they named *Band* (because of the tape) and -*Aids* (for first-aid).

Today, almost everyone uses Band-Aids for their cuts. But sometimes it's not your body that needs fixing. Maybe your feelings are hurt or your heart is sad, and your pain is on the inside. That's when only God can help. The Bible says, "He heals the broken-hearted and binds up their wounds" (Psalm 147:3, NIV). If you ask him to, God will cover your hurt with his love and protection until it is better—and he doesn't even need a Band-Aid!

7

How did a little girl's letter change history?

The little girl's name was Grace Bedell, she lived in New York, and when she was 11 years old she wrote a letter to a very famous man. The letter told this man that he should grow a beard. Grace thought his face was too thin and that he would look better with a beard. One day, when this man came to Grace's city on a train trip, he asked to see her. Grace went to meet him, and when he saw her, he gave her a kiss and said, "You see, I let the whiskers grow for you, Grace." Who was the man? You've seen pictures of him yourself. His name was Abraham Lincoln.

You can imagine that it was quite exciting for Grace to know that a president was listening to her. She couldn't help but feel important. But a president isn't nearly as powerful as God. Do you know what God thinks about children? Jesus explains to us how God feels.

Jesus says, "Beware that you don't look down upon a single one of these little children. For I tell you that in heaven their angels have constant access to my Father" (Matthew 18:10). God especially loves children, and he always listens to their prayers.

God wants you to know that you are very important to him and that he always has time for you. He will never be too busy to pay attention to your feelings. God gives you, his child, a special place in his kingdom. If you ever feel that your friends or parents aren't listening to you, or that you have problems that no one seems to be able to help you with, remember that you have someone on your side who will always make you his top priority. Tell God that you want him to be part of your life, and he will always be available for you to talk to him. You don't even have to write a letter to get his attention!

8
Why are barns red?

So many barns are red that you might think someone long ago said, "Red is a cheerful color. Let's all make our farms prettier by painting our barns red." But that didn't happen at all. Actually, the weather is responsible for barns being red.

Back in the 1700s, farmers needed to protect their wooden barns from the warping and rotting that different kinds of weather can cause. After experimenting, farmers found a good mixture to paint on their barns. It was made from skim milk, lime, and a chemical called iron oxide. When these three things were mixed together and spread on wood, they dried to a plastic-like coating that lasted a long time. The iron oxide in the mixture was a reddish color, and it turned the wood red. Since almost everyone used this mixture, red-colored barns sprang up everywhere. Soon people got so used to seeing them that red barns became the custom.

Barns are places people store crops and shelter animals. The Bible has something to say about filling barns. Barns are so large that it would take a long time to fill a barn completely from bottom to top. But God's Word tells us, "Honor the Lord by giving him the first part of all your income, and he will fill your barns with wheat and barley" (Proverbs 3:9-10). When you love someone, you want to share. That's why we give to God first whenever we earn any money. We might not need wheat or barley, but God knows just what we do need. And when we give something to God, he promises to give back more than he gets—enough blessings to fill up a whole barn!

9
Which sport started with a fruit basket?

Football was played in the fall, and baseball in the spring. What kind of indoor

ball game could be played in the winter? Dr.
James Naismith, who worked at a Massachu-
setts YMCA in the late 1800s, came up with
the answer.

Dr. Naismith nailed peach baskets to the
balconies on each end of the gym. Players
tried to throw an old soccer ball into the
peach baskets. Fans watching the games
sat in the balcony behind the baskets. To
help their favorites win, when a ball came
toward the basket, fans would slap the
ball, kick it, or even hit it with umbrellas
or sticks to help it land in the basket. Soon
wire was put behind the baskets so the
fans couldn't reach the ball. But when the
ball hit the wire, it bounced off to unex-
pected places. The wire backboard was
eventually changed to wood, and finally
to glass. The baskets themselves were
another problem. Janitors had to stand on
a ladder through the whole game to throw
the balls back out of the baskets! Soon a
hole was made in the bottom of the baskets so the ball would come out. Then a
trapdoor was made in the bottom of the
basket that would open when a rope was

pulled. Twelve years after basketball started, a net was made that the ball could fall through. The soccer ball was replaced with a bigger, lighter ball; and sneakers, which slid around on gym floors, were changed to shoes with better traction. Now players were ready to really play ball!

When you're young, God gives you lots of energy and the desire to jump and run and play until you've exhausted yourself. It's good for you to participate in sports, because that gives you the chance to use up energy in an interesting way. But God doesn't want you to get so involved in the game that you lose sight of him. He wants you to play honestly and fairly and with kindness to your teammates and your opponents. If you'll do anything to win, like cheating or injuring someone on purpose, you're not showing that God is the coach of your life. The Bible says, "Don't let the excitement of being young cause you to forget about your Creator" (Ecclesiastes 12:1). You're never too young to be a good example for God.

10

When did an umbrella make people laugh?

When John Hanway walked around London with his umbrella in the 18th century, he always caused a big commotion. Some people laughed at him. They made fun of him because at that time umbrellas were just for women. Umbrellas were mainly used to shade ladies from the sun and were made of colorful cloth and trimmed in gold or silver. In fact, the word *umbrella* comes from the Latin word *umbra,* meaning shade. The men of London thought John was being silly.

Other people got angry with John. Coach drivers were upset because they were afraid that if John showed people that they could walk in the rain, no one would pay for a carriage to take them anywhere. Church people said that John was being disrespectful, because they thought that when God made it rain, he wanted people to get wet.

John paid no attention to what people said. He carried his umbrella everywhere he went. When he had visited Portugal, John had learned that umbrellas were given to royalty as gifts and that whenever Portuguese sailors landed in another country, they would jump out of their ships and hold an umbrella up over their captain's head so everyone would understand that he was in charge. John Hanway liked the Portuguese ideas and decided to prove to the English people that umbrellas were for everyone, in all kinds of weather. Finally, after 30 years, lots of English people began to carry umbrellas, and John wasn't laughed at anymore.

John believed in the umbrella so much, he didn't pay any attention to the people who made fun of him. Sometimes, as God's children, we have to do the same thing. There are people who don't believe in Jesus. They want to make you feel bad. But stay strong, and don't pay attention. You can be proud to say to God, "I am mocked and cursed and shamed for your sake" (Psalm 69:7). God will protect you much more than the umbrella protected John.

11 Which president had a giant bathtub?

In the 1800s, if you wanted to take a bath, you probably had to go downtown to do it. Most homes had no bathtubs, so the city provided a bathhouse where you could get clean. If you *were* fortunate enough to have your own tub, you would have taken your baths in the kitchen, where most bathtubs were kept.

The first tubs were around seven feet long and could weigh as much as half a ton. The water for your bath came from the sink, but you had to heat it on the stove first before you poured it into the tub. Because it was expensive to fill up the tub, many people thought bathing was a luxury. So instead, they filled their tubs with dirt and grew vegetables and flowers there. The White House bathtub had to be made even bigger than normal because President Taft, who weighed

350 pounds, once got stuck in it. The president ordered a new tub that was so huge that when it was delivered, four grown men all climbed inside it at the same time and got their picture taken.

Imagine how good it felt to be clean in those days, whenever you finally did get around to taking a bath! Do you know that having God to make you clean inside feels even better than a bath? In the Bible, God says, "Come, let's talk this over! . . . no matter how deep the stain of your sins, I can take it out and make you as clean as freshly fallen snow. Even if you are stained as red as crimson, I can make you white as wool!" (Isaiah 1:18).

If he hasn't washed you clean yet, it's only because you haven't asked him to. God is waiting for you to come to him. How can you do that? Right now, right where you are, tell God that you want to be his child. Tell him you're sorry for the things you've done wrong, and ask him to let you start over, so that you can live out the plans he has for you.

12

Can you tell what a bird eats by looking at it?

The answer is as plain as the beak on its face! A woodpecker's beak is long and strong enough to peck through the bark of a tree and reach inside for insects. Birds who eat seeds need short beaks to crack them open. The beak of a bird that eats meat, like an eagle, has a hook in it. That helps the bird rip up the meat into pieces small enough to swallow. What about the beak of a pelican? This bird eats fish, and there is a big pouch under its bill so that it can catch a fish by scooping it into the pouch. That's how to get a clue about what a bird will do!

Different birds eat different foods, and God makes sure that the foods they need are nearby. Jesus tells us, "Look at the birds! They don't worry about what to eat—they don't need to sow or reap or store up food—for your heavenly Father feeds them. And you are far more valuable to him than they are" (Matthew 6:26). When you see birds today, remember that God is watching over you even more than he watches over them.

13
How was the toothbrush invented?

A prisoner, a bone, and a hog all helped to make the toothbrush. Long ago, before anyone had thought of a toothbrush, people kept their teeth clean by chewing on a stick until one end got soft and frayed like a brush. Sometimes they dipped a finger in chalk or salt and then rubbed their teeth. Toothpicks were another way to take care of teeth, and toothpicks were very fancy then. They were made of gold or jewels, and people would stick them in their hats or hang them on necklaces when they weren't using them. The first brushes came from China, where the Chinese made them out of hairs pulled from the backs of wild hogs. The invention of the toothbrush as we know it came from Joseph Addis. He worked on the toothbrush while he was in jail. First, he saved a bone from one of his meals and poked some holes in it. His prison guard gave him some bristles. Joseph tied the bristles into little bundles, cut them to make them even, put glue on the ends, and stuffed them into the holes.

Toothbrushes clean your teeth, but they don't do anything to improve the words that come out of your mouth. While you're making your teeth bright and shiny, think about polishing up what you say. The Bible tells you how to do it: "I will praise the Lord no matter what happens. I will constantly speak of his glories and grace. I will boast of all his kindness to me" (Psalm 34:1-2). Saying cheerful, encouraging, pleasant things will not only freshen your day, but everyone around you will feel refreshed, too.

14
What makes Mexican jumping beans jump?

First of all, it isn't really a bean. It's a seed. It comes from a shrub in Mexico. And it doesn't really jump. It rolls and tumbles because there is a moth larva, or caterpillar, inside. The caterpillar drilled a hole to get into the seed, where it eats the inside. Eventually, the caterpillar becomes a moth and crawls out the same hole it made to come in.

But before it goes to sleep, waiting to turn into a moth, it moves all around in the seed. Why? When the seed is in sunlight, it becomes too hot inside for the caterpillar. So the insect tosses and turns until it can feel that the seed has rolled into some shade.

When a cloud covers the sun, the caterpillar probably enjoys being able to rest for a moment, because there is shade everywhere. Then the cloud blows away, the sun comes back out, and the caterpillar must start rolling again. People like the sun much more than the caterpillar does. We're happy when clouds move away and the world gets bright again. God talks about clouds when he tells us how he gets rid of our sins. He says, "I have swept away your offenses like a cloud" (Isaiah 44:22, NIV). When you see a floating cloud, remember that the same God who sends the clouds skittering across the sky wants to dust your soul clean with just a puff of his holy breath. If you've never asked him to, why not ask him now?

15

What did a president of the United States, a candy seller, and a stuffed animal have to do with a favorite children's toy?

When Theodore Roosevelt was president, he went hunting one day. A bear was captured and tied up for the president to shoot, but President Roosevelt said he would not kill the bear. The story became famous when it was reported in the newspaper and drawn as a cartoon.

A man named Morris Michtom owned a stationery and candy shop. His wife, Rose, sometimes made little stuffed bears, which they would put in the window of their shop. The Michtoms saw the cartoon about the bear, and that gave Morris an idea. He asked his wife to make some special bears like the one in the cartoon. Then Morris wrote a letter to the White House, asking if the new bears could be named after the president. President Roosevelt wrote back to Morris and said, "I don't think my name is likely to be worth much in the bear business, but you are welcome to use it." So Morris put the new bears in his shop window, next to the cartoon. The stuffed bears were called by the president's nickname: "Teddy's bear." We call them *teddy bears* today.

It's fun to think about how names got started. Many times we don't even remember why we call something by a certain name. And sometimes names themselves get forgotten, too. But there is one name that will always be remembered. The Bible says, "Your name, O Lord, endures forever, your renown, O Lord, through all generations" (Psalm 135:13, NIV). Because people have told each other about God for thousands of years, you know who he is today. Tell others about Jesus, and pass his blessings into the future.

16

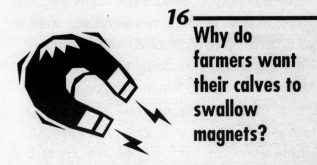

Why do farmers want their calves to swallow magnets?

Baby calves need to be looked after a lot. Their moms, the cows, must know this, because they take turns babysitting each other's calves. One cow will stay near a group of calves to watch them while the other cows graze farther away. After a while another cow will take over the baby-sitting job.

One thing the mother cows can't do is guard what their calves eat. For some reason, calves especially like to eat metal, like wire, staples, tacks, and nails. Farmers call this the "hardware disease," and they know how to solve the problem. When a calf is born, the farmer will often force it to swallow a magnet. All the metal that the calf eats will stay together in its stomach, stuck to the magnet.

The Bible says, "Be sure you know the condition of your flocks, give careful attention to your herds" (Proverbs 27:23, NIV). This is what the farmers are doing when they take care of their calves. Whenever you are in charge of something, especially when you're taking care of your pets, give each job your whole attention. Do your best at every task, and you will be pleasing God.

17

Can a beaver make a tree fall in just the right spot?

Lots of stories are told about the beaver, but not all of them are true. It is said that a beaver knows exactly where to chew a tree so that it will fall where the beaver wants it to. This is not true. The beaver doesn't have any idea where the tree will come down, and he has to be quick to get out of the way or risk getting hit. Another story about beavers says that they carry mud on their wide, flat tails to where the dam is being built, and then spread the mud with their tails. That's not true either.

Beavers do carry mud and sticks, but they hold their cargo against their bodies with their front paws. It is true that beavers use their tails to help steer themselves when swimming. And beavers do slap their tails on the water to warn each other of danger. Also, once dams are built, beavers always repair them immediately if they come apart.

Some mother beavers keep their babies inside "houses" made of mud and sticks. The doors are underwater, so only beavers can swim in. Beavers don't get splinters when they chew wood, because they chew only live trees that hold lots of sap. The branches are then kept under water, so the wood doesn't get dry enough to have splinters.

It's hard for us to understand how powerful God is and how he can take care of the whole world at the same time. As just one example, think about all the pets in your neighborhood. What if you had to take care of every one of them yourself? That would be quite a chore. Next, imagine that you were in charge of all the animals in your state—not just the pets, but also all the wild animals like the beavers, squirrels, rabbits, prairie dogs, and foxes. You would have to spend all your time feeding and watching over all these creatures.

Now think about God. He takes care of all the animals in your city, in our whole country, and all around the world—not just for one day, but every day and night. And besides that, God pays careful attention to each person on earth, too! The Bible says that God "constantly [satisfies] the hunger and thirst of every living thing" (Psalm 145:16). That's why we shouldn't worry about what will happen to us. Because God is in charge, we can be sure that he is always taking good care of his children in very loving ways.

18

Why keep a broken bell?

There was a big crowd in front of the State House in Philadelphia. The new bell had arrived from England, and it was about to be rung for the first time. The bellringer swung the clapper, the bell made a lovely bong, and then it cracked all the way up the side. Now it had to be fixed. A brassmaker named Mr. Stowe was hired to do the job. First, he melted the bell, and then he remolded it. The bell was tested again. This time it just went *thud* when it was rung, so back to the shop it went. Again it was remade, and again it was rung. Finally it was perfect—which was a good thing, because this became the Liberty Bell that was rung to gather everyone when the Declaration of Independence was read out loud for the first time.

In 1777, however, the Liberty Bell was in trouble again. Americans had to take it down and sneak it out of town at night to hide it from the British army, because the army would probably try to melt it and make bullets out of it. The bell stayed in the basement of a church for a year. Then it was brought back to Philadelphia and hung up again, to be used for important occasions for the next 57 years. But one day, something amazing happened when it was rung. The Liberty Bell cracked again! What was really surprising was that it broke on exactly the same day, July 8, as it had cracked the first time—59 years earlier. It hasn't been rung since then, but it has been visited and admired by many Americans.

Liberty is another word for freedom. Some people say that they don't want to be Christians because they would have no freedom— there are too many rules to follow. But this is not true at all! The Bible says, "Dear brothers, you have been given freedom: not freedom to do wrong, but freedom to love and serve each other. For the whole Law can be summed up in this one command: 'Love others as you love yourself'" (Galatians 5:13-14). When we follow this one rule, we have true freedom and live in a way that pleases God.

19

Why would anyone be accused of stealing their own car?

That's what almost happened to Richard Baker and his wife. After shopping, they unlocked their car in the parking lot and drove away. Richard noticed that his seat had been pushed back farther than he had left it, but he fixed it and forgot about it. Then his wife asked whose sunglasses were in the car. She found other things in the car that she didn't recognize, too. Finally she said, "This isn't our car!" Richard stopped the car, got out, and checked the license plate. She was right—it was someone else's car!

They drove back to the shopping center, where they saw the police in the parking lot. The police were talking to the owner of the car Richard and his wife were driving—everyone thought it had been stolen. Richard got out and explained that this car looked exactly the same as his car, and his key had worked in the lock. The policeman found that Richard's key worked in both cars, and so did the other owner's key. But the most amazing thing of all was that both men had the same last name—Baker—even though they had never met! And the whole mix-up happened on April Fool's Day!

Maybe sometimes you feel you are like one of those cars: that you are nothing special in God's eyes, and that he probably can't even tell you apart from anybody else. But you're wrong! God knows exactly who you are because he created you. We can say to God, "You made all the delicate, inner parts of my body and knit them together in my mother's womb" (Psalm 139:13).

God knew who you would become long before you were even born. He has given you a combination of talents and abilities that doesn't match anyone else's. God created you with everything you would need to become the special person that you are today. No one else on earth is exactly like you. God planned it that way, and that's why he loves you so much.

20
Why would a bird need goggles?

Your eyes water when they are hit by a strong wind. You might have wondered whether this happens to a bird's eyes when it flies. The answer is no, because a bird's eyes are made differently from ours. Birds have an extra eyelid that we don't have. This clear eyelid is close to the beak in the corner of each eye. When the bird is not flying, the eyelid just slides over the eye when the bird blinks, wiping away dirt and soothing the eye with oil. But this unique eyelid, called a *nictitating membrane,* does something special when the bird flies. It sticks in a closed position, covering the eyes like a pair of goggles. Since the nictitating membranes are clear, the bird can still see through them.

God gave eyes to birds, animals, and

people so that they could see where they are going. We learn to trust our eyes to give us information about the world. But God asks us to go a step further. He asks us to believe in him *without* being able to see him. The Bible says, "We live by faith, not by sight" (2 Corinthians 5:7, NIV). If you were blind and your friend took your hand and led you into the living room, you would have to trust her word that that's where you were standing. You couldn't use your eyes to see where you were. God says that we can trust what he tells us to be true. Let him lead you.

——————— 21
Why did a dog want to live in a graveyard?

Once there was a stray terrier named Bobby. He was adopted by Jock Gray, a policeman in Scotland, and as time went on, they were always seen together. When Jock died in 1858, Bobby was left all alone. The third day after Jock died, Bobby trotted up to the restaurant where he and Jock had often had lunch together. The owner threw him his usual biscuit, but Bobby didn't eat it. Instead, he carried his food back to Jock's grave and ate it there. Bobby came to the restaurant every day for the next 14 years, and he always took his food back to his master's grave. Because everyone admired his loyalty, the townspeople took care of Bobby. He was given a license and a collar, shelter when it was cold, and plenty of food. Bobby was also allowed to be at the churchyard whenever he wanted (which was all the time). And when he died, the townspeople buried him in the best place—next to Jock.

Bobby was amazing because he wouldn't leave the man he loved: even after death; even though he didn't have to stay; even though he was just a dog. God's love for us is much stronger than a dog's could ever be. The Bible tells us, "God so loved the world that he gave his one and only Son, that whoever believes in him shall not perish but have eternal life" (John 3:16, NIV). God loves you so much that he allowed Jesus to die—the biggest sacrifice that could be made—so

that you could become God's child. If you
want a best friend whom you can always
count on, tell him so. Invite God into your
heart right now, and you can have his loving
and faithful companionship from this
moment on.

22

Why did a cookbook include a recipe for an explosion?

Just because it's written in a book
doesn't always mean that it's true. People put
books together, and people can make mistakes. A big mistake was made in 1978.
A publishing company
named Random
House printed
a cookbook. In
the cookbook
was a recipe
for caramel

slices. In the recipe, something very important was left out. It was a simple ingredient—water. If you tried to make the recipe without water, the way it was printed in the book, the can of condensed milk in the recipe could explode. To correct their mistake, Random House asked for all 10,000 copies of the book to be returned. Hopefully, they received them all, or else a cook intending to make a treat for a surprise could have a bigger surprise than he expected!

No one knew that the mistake in the cookbook was there, but when it was found, the publisher wanted to change it. That's what we should do. Like King David in the Psalms, we should ask God, "How can I ever know what sins are lurking in my heart? Cleanse me from these hidden faults" (Psalm 19:12). God will help you see the things in you that he wants you to change—and with his help, you can!

23

Can someone be double-jointed?

You've probably heard someone say they're double-jointed because they can bend their fingers or toes in extraordinary ways. Since a joint is sort of like a hinge, to be truly double-jointed someone would have to have two of their bones fastened together by two different "hinges." That never happens. No one is really double-jointed. So why can they bend more than you? The joints (or hinges) between bones can bend because they are made of ligaments, which are tough tissues. Sometimes, these ligaments become permanently stretched. When that happens, the joint can bend farther than normal. That makes people think that they are double-jointed.

Speaking of joints, your jawbone has an interesting one. Maybe you assume that when you open your mouth, both your upper and lower jaw move. That's not true. The lower jaw is the only part that is movable. To test this, try to move your upper jaw while keeping the rest of your head still. It can't be done.

One last fact about bones that you may not know is that bones are *not* the hardest part of your body. Your tooth enamel—the white covering on your teeth—is harder than your bones; the difference is that a bone can grow to repair itself, but teeth can't.

The Bible tells us that if we belong to Jesus, "we are members of his body, of his flesh, and of his bones" (Ephesians 5:30, KJV). This is another way of saying that we are important to him, and he will take special care of us. No one wants to break a bone on purpose. We try to take care of our bones because they are important to our bodies.

24
How can you read when you can't even see?

Even a 16-year-old can change the whole world! Louis Braille did. And Louis had been blind since the age of three.

When Louis Braille was a small boy, he used to spend lots of time in his father's saddlery shop. One day, Louis snuck into the shop by himself and tried to copy what he had seen his father do, cutting leather with a sharp knife. The knife slipped, and Louis stuck himself in the eye. Eventually, his other eye became affected also, and he ended up completely blind.

Louis went to a school for the blind to try to learn to read, but it was very hard. There were only 14 books in the whole school, and they weighed 20 pounds each! The letters in these special books were just like regular letters, except much larger and puffed up from the page. Imagine having to feel the letter *w* with your fingers, or the letter *r,* or the letter *a,* and how long it would take to feel a whole word. But things changed when Louis was 15. A friend of the family, Charles Barbier, had invented a writing system using raised dots on paper. His soldiers needed to be able to read in the dark so the enemy wouldn't see them. Mr. Barbier came to get Louis's advice on his new writing system. Could Louis improve it? He did, by making the system simpler. Finally, there was a way for the blind to read, and it is named for the boy who figured it out: the Braille system.

If you close your eyes for 15 minutes, you will discover that being blind can be scary and dangerous. You need someone to help you. God says, "I will lead the blind by ways they have not known, along unfamiliar paths I will guide them" (Isaiah 42:16, NIV). You can depend on God to lead you in the paths he wants you to take, even if there are times that you can't see, or understand, what he's doing. He will lead you through what he says in his Word, the Bible, and also by what older Christians teach you—your mom and dad or your Sunday school teacher, for instance. God will never take you anyplace where you will be lost. He will always know exactly where you are, and he will be watching over you.

25

When do parents want their kids to make noise?

Imagine that you are a young African boy sitting in a tree house. You are beating on a drum made from a tin can with animal skin stretched over the top. You beat the drum all day because your father has asked you to. Are you in the tree house because you were making too much noise at home? No. Actually, you are doing a valuable job. When you beat your drum, you are scaring monkeys away from eating your father's crops.

As you get older in Africa, you will still be beating a drum, but now you will be making it talk. You will be given a special drum for sending messages. It is called a *lunga,* and it looks like an hourglass. You hold the lunga under your arm and squeeze it to make different sounds as you beat. Then you would learn to make your drum talk by hitting it with your hand, your fingers, or a drumstick. First, you have to learn the names of people in your family—each one has a different beat. Then you would learn to beat the names of all the leaders in your tribe. After practicing for a long time, you would be able to beat out words and sentences to send messages to other people in Africa who would be happy to hear your noise.

The most important message you can tell someone is that Jesus loves them. You can share with them the Good News of Jesus in what you say, or by your kindness, or through what you write, or even by beating a drum. Find a way to show someone how much God has blessed you, and start telling the story now. Then you can say, "O God, you have helped me from my earliest childhood—and I have constantly testified to others of the wonderful things you do" (Psalm 71:17).

———— 26

How could the idea of bungee jumping be over 100 years old?

Almost everyone has heard of the sport of bungee jumping, where a person fastens himself to a long rubber strap and jumps off some high place. The bungee jumper falls down fast, but the strap bounces him back up before he hits the ground.

Bungee jumping is not a modern idea. A Frenchman named Mr. Carron first thought of it in 1891. He made a metal case that could carry 15 people, so a whole group of people could ride at the same time. They each had their own cushioned chair to sit in, and on the floor was a mattress with bouncy springs almost two feet long. The capsule was going to be dropped from the top of the Eiffel Tower in Paris. On the ground below would be a 60-yard-deep pool shaped like a funnel.

Fortunately, no one ever took the capsule ride. Because this idea was planned by a human, it was likely to have many mistakes and could have been very dangerous. We get no guarantees with people—only with God. Christians say, "It is better to fall into the hand of the Lord (for his mercy is great) than into the hands of men" (2 Samuel 24:14). Be careful about trusting every word or idea people tell you. The best plan is to trust God first in everything.

27

If you burn your hand, what is the best thing to do?

Should you put ice on it, soak it in cold water, or smear it with butter? Butter is not the right answer, although lots of people think it is. Butter can have germs in it that might make the burn infected. Butter won't prevent a scar, either. Putting ice on it is also a wrong answer because ice can stick to your skin. The best thing to do for a burn is to run cool water over it, maybe for as long as an hour. Running water works better than soaking with water in a bowl. This is the best way to help prevent a scar and take the pain away. When your hand feels like it's on fire, think of a house that's on fire—what puts it out? Not ice, not butter, but water. You should do the same as the firefighters do, and run for the water.

When you burn yourself (which doesn't happen often) or when you are thirsty (which happens every day), you are happy to find water. The Bible tells us that learning about God is as satisfying as a glass of cool water when your mouth is very dry. Jesus says, "Let the thirsty one come—anyone who wants to; let him come and drink the Water of Life without charge" (Revelation 22:17). Just as our bodies would die without water, so our souls would die without God. Remember that God is ready and waiting to hand you an ice-cold drink of love every time you decide you are thirsty to learn more about him.

28

How did electricity surprise a whole crowd?

Imagine that you are in charge of getting people's attention at a fair. Electricity has just been invented, and most people are not used to seeing anything light up. What would really surprise them?

The Edison Electric Lighting Company thought of a good plan. They hired a man to hand out their business cards near the gate. What made this man special was that the Edison Company figured out a way to make the helmet he was wearing light up. The man had wires that ran underneath his jacket, connected to the helmet. Under the heels of his boots, he had some copper plates. There were also copper plates hidden in the ground underneath his feet. When the man stepped on these plates, touching them to the plates on his boots, his helmet lit up. The man secretly kept moving on and off the plates, making it look like his helmet went on and off all by itself. This was very shocking to people. At that time, because electricity was so new, it seemed like magic. Some people were so fascinated with the lighted helmet, they wanted to buy one to use around the house. They had no idea how complicated electricity really was.

Seeing an electric light for the first time must have been very exciting. Even though we see electricity all the time and are used to it, there is another kind of Light that can be very exciting. The Bible says, "The people who walk in darkness shall see a great Light" (Isaiah 9:2). If you tell someone about Jesus, and they have never heard of him before, it could be like turning on an electric light in a dark room. Tell the story. God will decide when to turn on the power in that person's life.

29

Why do boys' and girls' shirts button on different sides?

We all have buttons on our clothes. Have you ever noticed that boys' buttons are different from girls' buttons? It's not the size or shape or color of the buttons that makes them different—it's where they are. A boy's buttons are sewn on the right flap of his shirt, because most boys are right-handed and they use their right hand to button up. Girls' shirts have the buttons sewn on the left flap. Since most girls are right-handed, too, why are their buttons sewn on the left?

Long ago, buttons were very expensive, so only rich people had them on their clothes. Rich ladies did not dress themselves then; they had maids who got them dressed. The maid needed to have the buttons near *her* right hand as she stood in front of the lady to button her up, so the buttons were sewn on the left side. Even though most girls now dress themselves, the buttons have never been changed.

Both of your hands can be used for much more important things than buttoning. You can use your hands to help others. The Bible says, "When you give to the needy, do not let your left hand know what your right hand is doing, so that your giving may be in secret" (Matthew 6:3-4, NIV). This means that it is very important not to brag or show off when you are helping. Try to be so quiet about helping that no one even notices! Put away your little brother's toys, but don't mention it. If the trash can is full, empty it without being asked. Even if you don't get thanked or praised for your help, keep doing nice things. God will see you, and that's what counts.

━━━━━━━━━━━ 30
Why were M&M's invented?

Long ago, candy was just a small piece of a loaf of sugar, cut off with scissors.

Then candy got fancier, and people began making different kinds of candy for different reasons.

One favorite candy was invented during a war. Soldiers in 1940 needed a treat that they could carry in their pockets that wouldn't get their fingers sticky. Two men, Bruce Murrie and Forrest Mars, made a bite-sized chocolate candy that had a hard, colored coating. They named it after their initials: M&M's.

Other candies got their names from real people, too. Leo Hirschfield invented a chocolate candy and named it after his six-year-old daughter, Tootsie. The candy? A Tootsie Roll. Most people think that the Baby Ruth candy bar was named after the famous baseball player Babe Ruth. That's not the true story. This candy bar was named after a little girl, Ruth Cleveland. What made her special enough to have a candy bar named for her? She was the daughter of President Grover Cleveland.

You've probably told at least one of your friends how good one of these candies is. It's natural to want to tell someone else about good things! Then your friend learned the name and remembered it, too. That's how it is with Jesus. The Bible tells us that "God exalted him to the highest place and gave him the name that is above every name" (Philippians 2:9, NIV). People who hear about Jesus and get to know him grow to love him. Then they tell their friends about Jesus. When you tell someone the name of a new candy, you are sharing a sweet treat that lasts a few minutes. Telling your friends about Jesus can sweeten the rest of their lives.

How can you move an elephant?

— 31

It takes a long time to understand an elephant. That is why, in Asia, a young boy would be given his own baby elephant to make friends and be buddies with throughout his life. The boys would learn that elephants use their trunks like humans use their hands—the trunk is raised to say "hi," the trunk strokes another elephant when it's sick, or the trunk swings from side to side to show worry. Elephants talk, too—with snorts, growls, and squeaks—and each sound means something different. An elephant even blows its trunk like a horn to make people move out of the way. Elephants are very light sleepers—they sleep only about an hour a day. They snore very loudly when they do go to sleep.

After the boy learns these things, it is time for the elephant to learn from the boy. Riding on the back of his elephant, the boy teaches it that a touch on its back means *stop*, pressing its right ear means *turn right*, pressing its left ear means *turn left*, and a pat on the head means *kneel*. Now the boy-and-elephant team are ready to work.

The boy rides his elephant while the elephant pulls heavy logs from place to place or knocks over small trees. Elephants even used to be ridden into war like tanks. But elephants didn't do well in battle because they were too peaceful, would run away from a fight, and stepped on whoever was in their way, even their masters.

Training animals is a hard job, because you

are trying to make them do something that they're not used to doing. The Bible tells us, "Do not be like the horse or the mule, which have no understanding but must be controlled by bit and bridle or they will not come to you" (Psalm 32:9, NIV). This means that God wants us to come quickly and willingly to him. He doesn't want us to have to be dragged or pushed by our parents. Once you learn of God's greatness, run to him, because he will be waiting to show you his plan for you.

32

How did a toy stop an army?

Once, three little boys with a toy cannon stopped a whole army. Two groups of soldiers were practicing war games in Louisiana in 1944. The Blue Team was sneaking around in the woods. Nearby, three boys were playing with their toy cannon. It fired carbide gas and was very loud. The boys fired the cannon in the direction of the Blue

Team, not even knowing that they were there. The Blues heard the boom and didn't know who was shooting at them. They returned fire, shooting blanks (not real bullets) at the boys. The boys and the army shot at each other for almost half an hour. Finally, everyone discovered that 500 tanks, jeeps, and trucks, plus a lot of men, had been kept busy by three boys and a toy.

Sometimes you may feel like you are battling something much greater than you are, just like the boys were "fighting" against a whole army. Maybe it's your math class, or a school bully, or trying to learn to live with your parents' divorce. When you feel weak and powerless and unable to change things, turn your troubles over to God. God is stronger than any problem. The Bible reminds us how to count on him when it says, "The Lord is my Helper, and I am not afraid of anything that mere man can do to me" (Hebrews 13:6). God is mightier than anything on earth, even the biggest cannon ever built. He will bless you with hope, comfort, and help that go far beyond what any human could provide.

33

How did the propeller of a ship help invent the cash register?

It was because of a man named James J. Ritty, who owned a business in Ohio. Mr. Ritty had a big problem. He owned a store, and his employees were taking money that didn't belong to them. Mr. Ritty had no good way to keep track of the money his business was making. This upset Mr. Ritty so much that he took an ocean cruise to feel better.

While he was on the ship, Mr. Ritty noticed a machine that was counting how many times the boat's propeller went around. A counting machine was just what Mr. Ritty needed! He was so excited about it that as soon as the ship reached shore, Mr. Ritty turned right around and went home again without spending even one night of his vacation there. Soon Mr. Ritty had designed and started selling the cash register. Some registers were made with a bell that would ring every time the drawer was opened. Anyone trying to sneak money out of the drawer would suddenly have everyone else in the store looking at him. One kind of cash register was even called the "thief catcher."

God tells us that workers have the right to keep the money they have honestly worked for. Mr. Ritty was right to keep his employees from stealing his money.

When you have your first job, be the kind of worker your boss can trust, not someone he always has to keep an eye on. And if you're a boss yourself someday, be sure to treat your employees fairly. The Bible explains, "You shall not rob nor oppress anyone, and you shall pay your hired workers promptly. If something is due them, don't even keep it overnight" (Leviticus 19:13). Whether you grow up to be a boss or an employee, remember to respect the people who work with you, and give them what rightfully belongs to them.

What haven't you noticed when watching the clock?

34

We spend a lot of time looking at the faces of clocks. Here are some facts about clocks that you may not have noticed. Many clocks use Roman numerals to show the hour. In school, you are taught that the number 4 is written as IV. But look carefully at the number 4 on clocks or watches that have Roman numerals. Quite often, the 4 is written with four straight lines. Why? Long ago, a French king named Louis XV had a watch. Whenever he looked at it, he got the IV (for the number 4) and the VI (for the number 6) mixed up. The king sent his watch back to the watchmaker and asked that the 4 be changed to look different from the 6. Naturally, everyone wanted to copy what the king was doing, so many clocks and watches began to use the four lines instead of the IV, and the custom still exists.

Check the faces of clocks and watches that are being advertised in newspapers, on TV, or in stores. If the clock has hands, most likely you will see that the hands are set at 8:20 or at 10:10. Why do so many clocks say the same time? People have tried to make this story very mysterious. One rumor says that clocks are set at 8:20 because that is when President Lincoln died. But he was shot around 10 at night and died around 7:30 in the morning. The real reasons that clocks and watches so often say 8:20 or 10:10 are not very exciting. When the hands are placed in either of these positions, the clock looks more pleasing because it looks balanced. The other reason is that most watchmaking companies put their names near the bottom of the face. When the hands of the clock are set at 8:20 or 10:10, the name of the company is not covered up, and you can see it easily.

We use time to help keep our days in order. It would be very confusing if kids went to school and came home at a different time each day. Suppose there were no schedule for when your favorite TV show would come on! What if you never knew whether your next meal would be served in five minutes or five hours? God keeps his world in order by creating day and night, and winter and summer. The Bible says, "There is a right time for everything" (Ecclesiastes 3:1). Use time to help you keep track of what you're doing, and make sure to include time for God!

35

Why does a cat lick like that?

Cats have everything they need to set up their own laundromats. They lick their fur to clean themselves, and it works very well because of their tongues and their saliva. The saliva of a cat has a kind of detergent in it, which keeps their fur washed and smelling sweet. The cat's tongue is rough, so when the tongue rubs

over the fur, it pulls out dead hair and dirt.
But licking helps cats in other ways, too. The
saliva acts like a little shower when the
weather is hot, helping the cat stay cool.
Also, when the sun shines on a cat's fur, it
makes Vitamin B, which the cat digests from
licking itself. Licking fur also helps a cat to
hunt, because after licking itself, the cat gets
rid of its natural odor. When the cat, especially a wild cat like a lion, tries to hunt,
other animals can't smell it coming.

Cats clean only the outside of their bodies.
But people need to think about being clean
on the inside, too. That's where our hearts
and souls and feelings and personalities are.
It doesn't matter how neat and clean you are
on the outside—God looks inside. He checks
to see if you are loving and kind and honest.
That's what makes you bright and shiny to
him. The Bible tells us, "First clean the inside
of the cup and dish, and then the outside
also will be clean" (Matthew 23:26, NIV).
When you are full of God's love on the
inside, it will shine out of you, and you will
look wonderful.

36

When did a softball player catch a flying baby?

Tom Deal was disappointed in himself. One afternoon, Tom had been playing softball, and he had missed a fly ball that should have been easy to catch. Because Tom missed the ball, his team lost. When he went to sleep that night he was still thinking of that bad catch. The next morning, Tom had something else to think about. He heard crying, and when he looked out the window, he saw that a baby in the apartment across the street was crawling out onto the balcony. The balcony was on the third floor, and the baby was heading straight for the railing. Tom dashed across the street and rang and rang the doorbell, but nobody answered. When Tom looked up, he could see that the baby was crawling right through the railing! Tom stretched out his arms and leaped forward— just in time to catch the falling baby.

Years from now, no one will remember whether Tom caught the baseball or not. But that baby's family will always remember that Tom was there to save their child. Lots of times we feel like failures for little things that didn't work out right. But when we believe in Jesus Christ, we can be free from disappointment about things that really don't matter. That's because we've taken care of the most important thing. The Bible tells us, "The eternal God is your refuge, and underneath are the everlasting arms" (Deuteronomy 33:27, NIV). This means that God promises to catch us in his arms no matter what.

37
Since fish are always in schools, aren't they smart?

When fish travel in groups, we call that group a school. Maybe that's why we expect fish to be smart—but they really aren't.

A good place to go fishing is on a bridge, because fish are attracted to the water below bridges. The water there is shady and dark. Plankton, which is a kind of plant, collects on bridges under the water, so the fish have plenty to eat. Because bridges are usually built at the narrowest part of a river, fish enjoy the way the water flows faster there.

While you're hooking a fish and pulling it out of the water, the other fish are watching. Why don't they swim away so they won't get caught also? When they see a fish struggling, the other fish get upset and try to hide. That's when they seem smart. But as soon as you pull the fish out of the water and out of sight, within a minute the other fish forget about danger and come swarming back.

The Bible tells us it is smart to remember: "Yes, I will bless the Lord and not forget the glorious things he does for me" (Psalm 103:2). If you forget how good God has been to you, you might become afraid. You might think that God has left you all alone and that you have no one to protect you. But the

Bible tells you that you don't need to be afraid and that you can prove it to yourself by listing all the ways God has already helped you. If you don't forget like the fish do, you won't be hooked by fear.

38
How did the cavemen build their caves?

Did cavemen have to chip away rocks and dirt until they had a hole big enough to live in? Not at all. The only thing the cavemen had to do before they moved into a cave was to find one. So how did the caves get there in the first place? The rain made them! There is a soft rock called limestone that is full of tiny holes. Rainwater dribbled through those holes for thousands of years and washed away the rock in between the holes. Finally there was just one big hole, and the hole was full of water. After the water drained out, the cavemen moved in.

Having a house already made of stone was

convenient for the cavemen. Rocks are hard and sturdy, and that is why the Bible says, "Come to Christ, who is the living Foundation of Rock upon which God builds" (1 Peter 2:4). You can always count on the promises of Jesus. If you make your relationship with Jesus the most important thing in your life, God will build you strong and sturdy.

39
Why do chickens wear contact lenses?

Why would anyone buy contact lenses for a chicken? Contacts usually make vision better. But the contacts that chickens wear make their eyesight *worse*.

Chickens often fight with each other to try to establish who is boss and to pick on the weak chickens. To keep them from fighting, their owner will sometimes put contact lenses in their eyes to make the chickens' vision blurry. Then they don't know which other chickens they are looking at, and they don't attack each other.

Also, the chickens wearing contacts have to look at the ground very closely to find their food. When a chicken keeps its head down, that means it doesn't want to fight, so the other chickens tend to leave it alone.

Contact lenses affect the way a person (or a chicken!) sees with their eyes. But to see and understand things better with your *heart,* you need God's help. The Bible promises that the Lord "opens the eyes of the blind" (Psalm 146:8). If you are confused or doubting, it's as if your soul is blind to God's goodness. Ask God to help, and he will make his love clear to you. Try it and SEE!

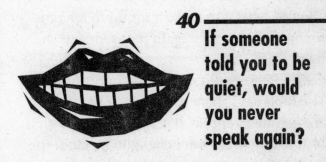

40

If someone told you to be quiet, would you never speak again?

Everyone has been asked to be quiet at one time or another, but Mrs. Regnier, a

French lady, didn't like being told to hush—she REALLY didn't like it. She had been speaking to her husband, and he said in an irritated way, "Be silent, woman, you talk nonsense." Mrs. Regnier got angry and left the room. She didn't speak to her husband for days.

Feeling bad, Mr. Regnier went to his wife and apologized. But she just stared at him and stayed silent. She wouldn't speak to anyone else either. When her daughter asked her for permission to marry, Mrs. Regnier wouldn't even say the one word *yes*. She just nodded to her daughter. After her one moment of anger, Mrs. Regnier never allowed herself to make a sound to anyone, for any reason, ever again for as long as she lived.

Mrs. Regnier did not do the right thing. The Bible says there is "a time to be silent and a time to speak" (Ecclesiastes 3:7, NIV). If Mrs. Regnier had been trying to be kind, she wouldn't have made everyone around her unhappy for so long. Her family wanted her to talk again, and they tried to tell her so. But she showed her family only selfishness instead of giving them love. If someone says something mean to you, don't say something mean in return. That is a time to be silent. As soon as you can, think of something nice to say and say it. That is when it's good to speak. Learning the right times will make you happy, and it will make other people happy with you.

41
How did chop suey get its name?

No one seems to know exactly who invented chop suey, but everyone agrees that it was first made in America. One story says that long ago, a Chinese diplomat was visiting the United States. Some of his American friends asked him to make a Chinese meal that they could sample. The Chinese man couldn't find the same ingredients in America that he had used when making meals in China, so he asked his cook to gather up some American foods and put them in a pot.

Then they added some tangy soya sauce (which not many Americans had tasted yet), served the dish, and created a taste sensation.

Another story suggests that a Chinese cook was feeding gold miners. He threw together all the leftovers, and chop suey was born.

And what about the name *chop suey*? There are several ideas about where the name came from. The *chop* could have come from chopsticks or from our English word *chop,* meaning to cut into small pieces. The *suey* could have started as a mispronunciation of "soya" sauce. Or the term *chop suey* might have come from the Chinese words *tsa sui,* which means a mixture of various bits and pieces and sounds like "chop suey" in English.

If you like to eat chop suey, then you're probably glad when you hear its name. The words *candy, present,* and *vacation* can make you feel happy, too. But words like *homework, shots,* or *punishment* might make you uncomfortable. When people hear your name, do they feel happy or angry? Do they like and admire you, or do they wish you would leave them alone? The Bible tells us that "a good name is better than fine perfume" (Ecclesiastes

7:1, NIV). When you act kindly and fairly, people will welcome you and your name, because you will be as pleasing to them as the most beautiful of perfumes.

42
Why did Cinderella wear glass slippers?

If you don't think being a good speller is important, consider the story of Cinderella. Because a bad speller made a small mistake, Cinderella ended up wearing the wrong shoes for the rest of history. In 1697, a Frenchman named Charles Perrault was copying the Cinderella story into his own language. In the earliest Cinderella stories, her shoes were made of gray and white squirrel fur. The French word for fur is *vair.* Charles wrote that Cinderella's shoes were made of *verre*, which sounds the same, but is spelled differently and means "glass." Ever since, American children have pictured the sparkling glass slipper left behind on the palace stairs and have wondered why they've never seen one.

When Charles made his spelling mistake, he probably had no idea that his mistake would become so famous. He would probably be embarrassed if he knew about it. The Bible says, "Whatever you do, do well" (Ecclesiastes 9:10). People often look at your actions to see what kind of person you are. So double-check that homework, and put some extra effort into your chores. Do your work so that your example will shine as much as that "glass" slipper did.

43
What made feeding babies more fun?

Before 1900, if you had a baby in the house, you had a mess in the kitchen. That's because you had to strain your baby's food before every meal so as to make it mushy enough to be eaten without teeth. Dorothy and Dan Gerber were tired of fixing meals for their baby, Sally, but store-bought baby food could only be bought with a prescription and was very expensive. Sally's grandfather owned a vegetable canning plant, so her parents suggested to him that they begin making their own foods. The first five kinds were peas, spinach, prunes, carrots, and vegetable soup.

The Gerbers were pleased with the new products and knew that other parents would buy them if they just knew about them. So Dan came up with an idea to help sell the baby food. He put a notice in *Good Housekeeping* magazine. He made an offer to parents, telling them that they could buy six jars of baby food for only one dollar if they would send in the name of their grocer. Dan then went to each grocery store and showed how many people had sent in the grocer's name, people who would buy the baby food if they could find it in the store.

Then the Gerbers had a contest to see who could draw a healthy, happy baby to use as the picture on the Gerber baby food jars. One lady, Dorothy Hope Smith, decided to send in a drawing, but she didn't finish it. She told the Gerbers she would work on it some more if they wanted to use it. But the Gerbers loved the drawing just the way it was, and they used the drawing on every jar. And there were a lot of jars—the Gerbers eventually made more than 187 kinds of foods for babies.

A baby trusts his parents to feed him only what is good for him. The baby doesn't ask questions or examine the food—he just opens his mouth. As God's children, we can have that kind of faith in him. It pleases him for us to say, "O Lord, you alone are my hope; I've trusted you from childhood" (Psalm 71:5). No matter how old you get, God wants you to accept every blessing he sends with the complete trust of a baby taking food from a spoon.

44

How did people wake up on time before alarm clocks?

How would your family wake up on time without an alarm clock? Long ago, there was no such thing, so inventors worked on different ways to get people to open their eyes. Many things were tried, like a machine that sprinkled cold water on the sleeper, or a bed that tipped up and slid the sleeper out. Monks would light a candle and stick it between their toes before going to sleep. When the candle had burned down far enough for the flames to touch their toes, the monks knew it was time to wake up.

In 1882, Samuel Applegate thought there must be a way to be awakened more pleasantly. His idea was to attach a cord to a clock. When the time was right, the clock would release the cord, which ran to a big frame hanging over the bed. Dangling from

the frame were 60 corks, which dropped
onto the sleeper.

Many of us don't like getting up, but we
miss a chance to start the day with God
when we're grouchy. The Bible tells us,
"Arise, my people! Let your light shine for all
the nations to see! For the glory of the Lord
is streaming from you" (Isaiah 60:1). God is
happy when we are cheerful, because that
means we are so full of his love that we have
some extra to give away. Start someone's day
by giving them a smile, and your day will go
better, too.

45
How can you tell where a coin was made?

If you want to find out where a coin
was made (or *minted*), here's how you can do
it: If the coin has a little letter *D* stamped on
it, the coin was minted in Denver. An *S*
means it came from San Francisco. If there is

no small letter on the coin, it was made in Philadelphia.

Here are some more fun facts that you may not know about our coins:

Every face on every United States coin is always turned to the left. The one exception is the penny, on which President Lincoln's face is looking to the right.

The penny and the nickel have smooth edges, but dimes and quarters have grooves around theirs. There is a reason for this. Long ago, coins were made of valuable metals like gold and silver. Dishonest people sometimes tried to carve some of the metal off coins before spending them. That meant that they weren't paying the storekeeper as much metal as he was supposed to get. It was a way of cheating. Pennies and nickels were not made of valuable metals, but dimes and quarters had real silver in them. So the government put notches on the edges of dimes and quarters. If anyone tried to shave some of the silver off, it would show, because the grooves would be gone. Just in case you're wondering, quarters have 119 notches, and dimes have 118!

Sometimes people make the mistake of

thinking their money is the most valuable thing they have. But that's not true. Jesus wants to give us much more than money. If you belong to him, you have his gift of heaven and his love. You have talents that he has given you. You have kindness and cheerfulness to give away to others, and those qualities can't be priced. They may be the most valuable presents that someone receives on a day when they are discouraged. When a poor man asked the apostle Peter for money, Peter told him, "Silver or gold I do not have, but what I have I give you" (Acts 3:6, NIV). Share your heart, share your helping hands, and share your caring. Those are the possessions that make you truly rich!

46
Why aren't there more green flowers?

We enjoy the pretty colors of flowers, but the colors are not there just to please us.

They have a more important purpose. To make more plants, pollen has to be carried from one flower to another flower just like it. Flowers need insects to step on them so that the pollen will stick to their feet and come off on the next flower they land on. Their bright colors help attract insects. Bees like yellow and blue flowers. Butterflies are attracted to all bright colors. The plants that flower at night usually have very pale blooms so that moths can see them in the dark. Not many insects or birds are attracted to the color green, so there are not many green flowers.

It is exciting and pleasing to us when a garden grows. The Bible tells us, "The Lord will show the nations of the world his justice; all will praise him. His righteousness shall be like a budding tree, or like a garden in early spring, full of young plants springing up everywhere" (Isaiah 61:11). God's garden of love will attract even more people than a flower garden does. God used one of the most beautiful places on earth, a garden, to describe for us how wonderful the world will be one day, when everyone will know about him.

——————————————**47**

Are you feeling red, pink, or yellow today?

You may not realize it, but colors can affect the way you feel. Scientists have tested people's reactions to colors, and they found some interesting results. Yellows and oranges make people feel happier, warmer, and more active. Red is an even stronger color in this group; in fact, red is such a strong color that it can make some people feel nervous. Blues and greens are calming colors. They make your blood pressure, heart rate, and breathing go slower. Another powerful color for making you feel peaceful and quiet is pink.

If you were decorating a fast-food restaurant, which colors would you choose to use? The next time you go for a hamburger or a pizza, notice the walls and decorations—even the signs out in front of the restaurant. Most fast-food places stay away from greens, pinks, and blues, because these colors make people, as well as their appetites, slow down. Oranges and yellows are the best colors to inspire people to eat a lot, eat faster, and leave sooner; that way, there is room for even more customers to come in and do the same thing.

Colors may temporarily change our moods, but there is something much more lasting than paints or crayons to change our personalities. God wants to change you for good. The Bible tells us, "He turned my sorrow into joy! He took away my clothes of mourning and clothed me with joy" (Psalm 30:11). If something is bothering you, don't just look for a cheerful room to make you feel better. That won't work for very long. Instead, take your problem to God. When he helps you, it's for good.

48 What bird gives its babies up for adoption?

One day, a cardinal was sitting on her eggs in her nest. She flew away for a moment, and when she came back to her nest, there was an extra egg in it. She didn't seem to notice, and she sat on all the eggs anyway. That was good news for another bird called the cowbird. Cowbirds never build nests of their own, and they never help raise their own families. Instead, they sneak into other birds' nests and lay their eggs there. Baby cowbirds hatch faster than most other birds, so the tiny cowbird is often the first chick the foster parents see. The parents feed the cowbird even though it doesn't look like the other babies.

The cowbird didn't take care of her baby herself, but she made sure that someone else would. That baby bird would grow up never knowing its real parents, but it would still be provided for. These birds have shown us something about God's love. The Bible tells us, "If my father and mother should abandon me, you [God] would welcome and comfort me" (Psalm 27:10). Maybe some of your friends have only one parent or don't even live with their mom or dad. You can tell them that God wants to be their Father. He wants to take good care of them and give them all the love they have been missing. Just as the cowbird grows up and has someone to take care of it, even without its parents, so your friends can learn to live a happy life leaning on God's love.

49
Why do golfers yell *fore?*

When you're out on a golf course, you will hear a lot of golfers yelling the word *fore* and then hitting the ball. Why did they pick the number four, and why aren't they getting in trouble for screaming it?

Actually, it doesn't mean a number at all. Golfers are really copying something soldiers from long ago used to do. Soldiers had to stand in rows when they shot their guns at the enemy in a war. The back row of soldiers needed to warn the soldiers in the front row to move out of the way so they wouldn't get hit by bullets from behind. The soldiers would yell, "Beware before!" which meant "Get out of the way or you'll be shot!" Then the front row would kneel down, and the back row could shoot over their heads. But after a while the soldiers got tired of yelling the whole warning, so they shortened it to "Before!" and finally to just "Fore!" So when a golfer swings at the ball, he will yell "fore" to say, "Everybody, get out of the way of my golf ball, just in case it might hit you!" This is one time when it isn't considered rude to shout; instead, it's the most polite thing to do.

The Bible says, "The Lord will go before you, the God of Israel will be your rear guard" (Isaiah 52:12, NIV). When you are God's child, it is better than having a whole row of soldiers behind you to protect you. Because God loves us, he gave us the Bible to tell us every way to keep ourselves safe. The Bible doesn't shout, but what it has to say is loud and clear.

50

What happens when you grab a crab?

When you go for a walk on the beach, you're likely to find several empty crab shells on the shore. You might wonder what caused so many crabs to die. The truth is, nothing did. Each shell is like an empty house that a crab has already moved out of. Crabs grow bigger all the time, and their shells are too hard and stiff to stretch. The crab becomes really cramped and finally has to push off its old shell and grow a new one that fits him better. But the shell isn't the only part of a crab that can come off. Crabs can do a special trick to help protect themselves. If you grab a crab by one of his legs, he will just drop it off in your hand and scurry away. He can always grow a new one.

God's design for the life of a crab is fascinating. He gave each crab a sense of how to survive best. But crabs are not nearly as important to God as we are. He has made even more careful plans for our lives. The

Bible reminds us, "Not one sparrow (What do they cost? Two for a penny?) can fall to the ground without your Father knowing it. And the very hairs of your head are all numbered. So don't worry! You are more valuable to him than many sparrows" (Matthew 10:29-31). If God is paying so much attention to how a little bird flies or where a little crab lives, imagine how much more he cares about you, his child! God knows so much about you that he even keeps track of how many hairs you have. Even you don't know that number, and it's your own head! Have faith that God knows more about you than you know about yourself and that he is always watching over you with love.

—————— 51
What's the fastest-growing plant in the world?

If you've ever planted a garden, you know that it sometimes takes a lot of patience to wait for the plants to grow. It might surprise you to know that in Brazil there is a fungus, which is a kind of plant, that takes only 20 minutes to be full grown. This fungus is called the stinkhorn, and it starts its growing by absorbing water extremely quickly. The water fills up the dried-up fungus so fast that if you're standing nearby, you will hear a crackling noise while the fungus grows about an inch every five minutes. But that isn't the only unusual thing about the stinkhorn. Immediately after it finishes growing, the fungus starts to rot. Rotting is the fungus's way of spreading its seeds. The bad odor attracts flies, and the flies crawl on the fungus, where spores stick to their feet. Wherever each fly goes next, another fungus will begin.

It's fun and exciting when you don't have to wait for something. But things in real life usually take a lot longer to develop than the stinkhorn does. Most of the time we need to be patient. Having patience is a good thing to practice. The Bible says, "Be patient, like a farmer who waits until the autumn for his precious harvest to ripen" (James 5:7).

If you are praying for something to happen, wait for God's answer. There will be one, even though it may not happen as fast as you would like. God knows what answer you need to have. You can trust that he always hears you and that he always answers at the best time and in the best way.

How did frogs fall from the sky?

52

When it hails, it's hard enough to keep from getting hit by the "ice rocks" that are falling from the sky. But what if you had to dodge falling frogs, too? That's exactly what happened one day in Iowa in 1882.

During a hailstorm, the air is very cold up in the clouds, so the raindrops freeze and come down as ice pellets called hail. Meanwhile, strong winds are blowing up and down between the earth and the sky. On this day, the wind blew so hard that it picked up some small frogs and whisked them into the clouds. The raindrops began to freeze on the frogs, and they were coated with ice until they turned into hail as big as five inches across. Then the froggy ice cubes fell back to earth, where the amazed people of Iowa discovered them.

Finding that they were up in the clouds probably made the frogs pretty confused! Frogs are jumpers, but they had definitely never jumped *that* high before. Sometimes we are like those frogs. We get used to being ordinary and doing things the same way everyone else does them. When we have a chance to do something special, or we get an idea that no one else has ever thought of, we tell ourselves, *Oh, I'm sure I could never do that. No one else has ever done it before.* And we give up before we've even tried.

Whenever you get a different kind of idea than you've had before, remember that God may be giving it to you as a challenge to use your talents in a new way. If God could lift those frogs into the clouds, he can help you to be the first person who lives on the moon or the person who invents ice cream that doesn't have to be frozen. The Bible says, "Do not neglect your gift" (1 Timothy 4:14, NIV). Maybe the only reason it's never been done before is that no one else has the special abilities God has given you!

—————————— **53**

Why would a man be glad to live in a cabinet?

Patrick Fowler lived in a cupboard, which is a type of cabinet, and it saved his life. The cupboard was less than six feet high, and he stayed inside it for four years. Patrick was an English soldier stationed in France during World War I, fighting against the Germans. He got separated from the rest of his army and had to wear an ordinary coat instead of a uniform to disguise himself as he walked around. If the German soldiers noticed him, he would be killed.

A French woodcutter saw Patrick and decided to help him. He was allowed to hide in a cupboard in someone's house. Patrick came out of the cupboard only at night to eat, stretch, or go to the bathroom. Sometimes German soldiers insisted on visiting the house to drink coffee, but they never knew that Patrick was in there. Once, when the owners of the house had to move, a German soldier helped carry the cupboard. He didn't even notice how heavy it was or that Patrick was still inside it. Another time, the Germans began to search for enemies, and Patrick had to disguise himself as a woman of the village so the soldiers wouldn't find him. Patrick ducked under a haystack to hide. The soldiers stabbed the haystack with pitchforks, but they missed Patrick. The Germans finally retreated from France, and after four years of hiding, Patrick was safe at last.

Patrick needed the cupboard to stay safe. But the door could have broken, or the wood could have rotted away, or his hiding place could have been destroyed by fire. And then Patrick wouldn't have been safe anymore. The Bible tells us that we have much more than a piece of furniture to depend on: "For we know that if the earthly tent we live in is destroyed, we have a building from God, a house not made with hands, eternal in the heavens" (2 Corinthians 5:1, NRSV). That means that no matter what happens to us or our bodies on earth, if we belong to God we have the promise of living with him in heaven forever. Man could never build a place as wonderful as heaven, and man can't destroy what is waiting for us there. Only God could make such a perfect place where we can always feel peaceful and protected.

54

Did George Washington really have wooden teeth?

Imagine that you had only one tooth in your mouth. If you were a baby, it probably wouldn't matter. But what if you were a grown-up? That's what happened to George Washington. His teeth started falling out when he was about 22, and he had only one left by the time he became president. President Washington tried many different ways to replace his teeth. Although he never had wooden teeth, which is a story many people have heard, he did have teeth carved from elk's teeth or ivory. There were hinges between the top and bottom sets, and he had to bite down all the time just to keep his mouth from flying open. It was hard to talk and hard to eat. Once, President Washington had a set of dentures with a special hole so that the one tooth he still had could poke through. He tried to keep them smelling clean by soaking them in wine, but instead the fake teeth just turned black and got mushy. In 1796, the dentist had to pull out President Washington's last tooth, and the president kept his tooth in a gold locket attached to his watch chain. When the time came for the president to have his portrait painted, cotton was pushed under his lips so that he would look like he had teeth. But the cotton made his mouth puff out too far. Look at the picture on a dollar bill, and you can see for yourself.

What can we learn from George Washington's troubled teeth? The Bible mentions bad teeth when it says, "Putting confidence in an unreliable man is like chewing with a sore tooth, or trying to run on a broken foot" (Proverbs 25:19). That means that if we depend on someone who can't be trusted, we could be hurt or disappointed. And even trustworthy people will sometimes let us down. We should depend most on God to help us. He'll never let us down!

55
Why do we call it the "funny bone" when it definitely isn't?

Not only is it not funny, it's not even a bone! Along the upper arm bone, there's a nerve that runs underneath the arm. When it reaches the elbow, the nerve is very close to the skin. When you bump your elbow, you hit the nerve, and that is why it hurts. The upper arm, where the nerve is, has a big bone that's called the *humerus* bone. The name of the bone sounds the same as the word *humorous,* which means funny. People used to believe that it was the "humorous" bone that hurt when it was hit, so it got nicknamed the funny bone.

The first time you heard someone say he bumped his funny bone, you probably wondered how it felt. You might even have wanted to bump your own because it sounded like fun. The Bible tells us, "A cheerful heart is good medicine, but a crushed spirit dries up the bones" (Proverbs 17:22, NIV). It is good for us to be cheerful and to laugh. We like the feeling of being happy. So go ahead—have a few chuckles. But don't expect to get them from hitting your funny bone!

56
Which dogs were asked to dinner?

If you were ever invited to eat dinner in Paris with a very wealthy man named

Lord Egerton, you would be in for a big surprise. Lord Egerton always had 12 guests for dinner, and every one of his guests had four legs!

Lord Egerton loved his dogs and insisted that they eat at the table with him. Twelve dogs sat in 12 chairs with napkins tied around their necks. The dogs were very well-behaved, because they had been trained to have the same table manners as people. If one of the dogs forgot to be polite at the table, the next night it had to eat alone in another room. Its chair stayed empty until it showed it was sorry for misbehaving, and then it was allowed to return to its seat. After dinner, Lord Egerton would go for a ride in his carriage, and the dogs would go, too. But even then the dogs got special treatment, because they each wore four little boots to keep their feet from getting muddy. Lord Egerton's story is funny because he pampered his pets a little too much by treating them like people. But the Bible tells us, "A good man is concerned for the welfare of his animals" (Proverbs 12:10). God expects us to be kind to all of his creatures. Do your best never to injure or neglect your pet, but don't worry too much about teaching him to use a fork. Your pet would probably be just as pleased with a nice pat.

57
Did you know that you've probably used a cup named after a doll factory?

Long ago, when people were away from home and wanted a drink of water, they could go to the middle of their town, where there would be a large tub full of water with a big spoon to scoop and drink from. Everyone used the same dipper, so it was never very clean. A young man named Hugh Moore had an idea about how to fix this problem. He invented a machine that would give people a drink of water with a fresh cup each time for a penny. But people didn't use Hugh's machine, because they couldn't understand why they should pay for water when they could already get it free from the tub. Finally, laws were passed making it illegal to drink from dippers and spread germs and disease. Hugh Moore saw then that he didn't need to sell fresh water anymore; what people really needed were his paper cups. He began selling them to restaurants and soda fountains, and even to ice cream factories so kids could have a small cup of ice cream all to themselves. As his cups became more famous, Hugh began to look for a catchy name for them. Next door to his business was a doll factory. He asked the doll maker if he could borrow the name, and the doll maker said yes. That is why, when you use a paper cup, you will probably be drinking from a Dixie cup, which got its name from the Dixie Doll Company.

Our bodies need water to stay alive. If we had to find a new place to get water every day, we would be worried all the time about where our next drink would be coming from. God understands how hard that would be. That's why he says, "You shall be like a watered garden, like a spring of water, whose waters never fail" (Isaiah 58:11, NRSV). God is telling us that when we depend on him, we don't need to worry. He will make sure we always have what we need.

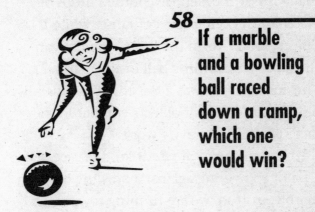

58
If a marble and a bowling ball raced down a ramp, which one would win?

We all know that a bowling ball weighs more than a marble. If you drop them both at the same time from a tall place, which would reach the ground first? An Italian scientist named Galileo wondered about this question. He decided to do tests to find the answer. But he lived so long ago, there wasn't a stopwatch to use as a timer. Everything that was dropped down would fall too quickly to measure. How could he make a decision? Galileo decided to roll things down a ramp to see which ones won the race. He understood that gravity, which is the force that pulls things toward the earth, would pull the same on big or small items. Galileo made his own timer: He counted drops of water as they fell into a container while objects rolled down the ramp. Which won the race—the bowling ball or the marble? The answer is—it was a tie, and it always will be, no matter which objects you put in the race. That's how gravity works.

Christians run a different kind of race. We are not competing against a bowling ball or a marble; instead, we are running toward the goal of becoming more like Jesus and eventually going to live with him in heaven. The Bible says, "Therefore, since we are surrounded by so great a cloud of witnesses, let us also lay aside every weight and the sin that clings so closely, and let us run with perseverance the race that is set before us" (Hebrews 12:1, NRSV). We need to drop the heavy sins that hold us back, and race on, letting nothing stop us until we cross the finish line in heaven.

59
Who had the biggest dollhouse ever?

Queen Mary loved to play with doll-houses when she was a little girl. But she was 57 years old when she got the best dollhouse of all as a present. The people of her country, England, spent four years and one million dollars to build it. The dollhouse is over eight feet long and five feet deep, and it has three stories. Everything in the house is very tiny, but it really works. Hot and cold water runs out of faucets made of real silver. Pieces of hot coal heat the ovens in the kitchen. An elevator goes up and down, light switches turn on the lights, and each door has a key that really locks it. Copies of the famous royal jewels are kept in a safe that can only be opened if you know the combination. A record player plays records one inch across; cars that really run, including a Rolls-Royce, are in the garage; and a drawer underneath the dollhouse has a pop-up garden. Lots of workers carefully built Queen Mary's doll-house, which is still kept at Windsor Castle where everyone can enjoy looking at it.

Jesus said, "In my Father's house are many rooms" (John 14:2, NIV). He was talking about heaven, God's house. If Queen Mary's amazing dollhouse was made here on earth by just humans, imagine what God's house must be like! After all, Queen Mary ruled only the small country of England—God is the King of the whole universe, including the land, the oceans, and even the stars. Think about the most wonderful place you can picture, and then remember that heaven will be even better than that!

60
When did a dog deliver mail?

Mail carriers usually have to watch out for dogs, to keep from getting bitten while trying to deliver the mail. But it's not often that the mail carrier IS a dog. That's what happened in the 1800s in Calico, California. One day, the town's postmaster found a black-and-white stray shepherd dog, whom he adopted and named Dorsey. Dorsey would follow the postmaster from house to house whenever it was time to deliver the mail. When the postmaster got sick and couldn't go on his mail route, he got an idea. He made two saddlebags for Dorsey that draped across the dog's back. He attached a note to Dorsey's collar, asking people to please put their mail in Dorsey's pouches. Then the postmaster sent Dorsey out. Sure enough, Dorsey went to all the right addresses. After that, Dorsey got a mail route of his own. Although he was a friendly dog, he would never stop to play until his letters were delivered!

We can learn a good lesson from Dorsey. Because he loved his master, he wanted to help. If you love Jesus, you will want to help him—and help other people, too. The Bible tells us, "Take tender care of those who are weak" (1 Thessalonians 5:14). If you can help a weak or sick person with a chore, do it. Volunteer even if you haven't been told—some people are too shy or embarrassed to ask. Helping others is a great way to show Jesus that you love him.

———————— **61**

Why do giraffes have such long necks?

A giraffe can see an enemy coming from far away because its eyes are so high up. Because the giraffe can reach far above where most animals can, it usually has plenty of leaves to eat from the tops of trees. The only trouble a giraffe has with his long neck is bending down to drink. To reach the water with its mouth, the giraffe spreads its front legs far apart and lowers its head between them. Giraffes must stay on guard against enemies, so they almost never lie down. Giraffes only get about 20 minutes of deep sleep by taking five-minute naps several times throughout the night. When baby giraffes are born, they fall five feet to the ground, but they are not hurt. In fact, a baby giraffe is standing up within 30 minutes, and running with the other giraffes when it's only about about 10 hours old! Don't worry about the little giraffes being too small to take care of themselves—young giraffes grow incredibly fast, sometimes as much as a whole inch in just two hours!

God gave the giraffe a way to get close to the tasty leaves at the top of a tree. We don't need leaves to eat, but we do need God's love, and Jesus gave us a way to get close to God. The Bible tells us that "in him and through faith in him we may approach God with freedom and confidence" (Ephesians 3:12, NIV). Having Jesus in our hearts is like having someone to lift us up to the treetops, even right up to heaven, so that we can get as close to God as we want!

━━━━━━━━━━━━━━━━━━ 62

How was a sinking ship saved by a comic book?

In 1964, a cartoon character saved a real ship from sinking. It wasn't Popeye who lifted the ship out of the water, or Superman who blew it to shore. The heroes of this story were Donald Duck and his nephews Huey, Dewey, and Louie.

A ship was coming into the harbor near Kuwait, getting ready to unload the 6,000 sheep it was carrying, when it began to sink. The people on land were very worried that the sheep would drown in the water and make it too dirty for drinking. There didn't seem to be any way to stop that from happening. Then a man named Karl Kroyer remembered a comic book he had read. In the book, Donald Duck and his nephews had found a sunken yacht and had brought it to the top of the water by filling it with Ping-Pong balls. Karl decided that this plan was worth trying. So he had 27 billion plastic balls stuffed into the bottom of the ship. Amazingly, the ship stopped tilting and floated safely to shore. Donald Duck saved the day!

Karl Kroyer probably got a lot of admiration for being able to control the ship. But imagine if he had been able to control the ocean! God is "mightier than all the breakers pounding on the seashores of the world!" (Psalm 93:4). Only God can control the sea. Not only that, but God invented the ocean in the first place. He made every grain of sand on its shores, and he even knows exactly how many grains there are. That's a lot more amazing than Ping-Pong balls!

63
Who was Chester Greenwood, and why did he cover his ears?

Chester Greenwood just had to do something about his ears. They were embarrassing him because whenever it got cold (which happened often in Maine, where he lived) they would turn unusual colors like red, white, purple, or blue. Not only that, but he couldn't even try out the new ice skates he'd gotten for his 15th birthday because his ears hurt when they got too cold. Chester had tried wrapping a scarf around his head, but it was scratchy. He needed to come up with a better idea. Here is what Chester thought of next: He twisted some wire so that it went across the top of his head, and made a loop on each end near his ears. Then he asked his grandmother to sew some material onto the loops. She put black velvet on the inside by his ears, and beaver fur on the outside of each loop. She sewed the wire across Chester's hat to make it stay. When Chester went out to ice-skate, his ears stayed covered up and toasty for the first time. Soon lots of people in his town wanted ear warmers like Chester's, and he finally had to open a factory when he was 19 just to make them all. Chester never dreamed that his funny ears would make him famous as the inventor of earmuffs!

God gave us ears for many good reasons. But one thing God *doesn't* want us to use our ears for is listening to gossip. If a friend tries to tell you a story about someone else, don't listen. Tell them you'd rather not hear it. The Bible says, "A gossip separates close friends" (Proverbs 16:28, NIV). Help your friends to stop gossiping about each other by refusing to listen, even if you have to wear earmuffs in the middle of summer!

64
When does a board game take a test?

It's the middle of winter, and you've been stuck in the house for days because of rain or snow. Christmas has come and gone, you're tired of playing with your new toys, and you're really bored. You happen to see a television commercial for a new board game, and all of a sudden it seems to be a terrific idea to buy one. Your attention wasn't grabbed by chance—it was done on purpose.

Toy companies know that after Christmas, it's hard to sell new toys. So that's the time toymakers concentrate on trying to sell board games to the bored. But not just any board game will do. The Milton-Bradley Company actually makes a game pass a test before the company will start selling it. Here are the things that Milton-Bradley wants to know: Is playing the game fun? Does the game have a reward at the end? Is the game too easy, so that it's not enough of a challenge? Is it so hard that players will get frustrated and want to quit? Will people want to play it more than once? If the game passes these tests, the company will try testing your willpower to see if they can persuade you that it's a game you just have to buy.

Games aren't the only things that need to be tested. The Bible tells us to test things we hear to see whether they're true or not: "Don't always believe everything you hear just because someone says it is a message from God: Test it first to see if it really is. For there are many false teachers around, and the way to find out if their message is from the Holy Spirit is to ask: Does it really agree that Jesus Christ, God's Son, actually became man with a human body? If so, then the message is from God" (1 John 4:1-2). Get to know God's book, the Bible, and then you won't be tricked.

65 How did they build a bridge across Niagara Falls?

Once there was a kite that helped build a bridge. It's true! Between Canada and the United States is a wide waterfall called Niagara Falls. It flows so swiftly that it's like 15 million water hoses shooting out their fastest water. Long ago, before there were so many buildings and so much traffic, people could hear the water whooshing down from as far as 20 miles away. Around 1848, people decided they needed a way to get across Niagara Falls to the other side.

They needed a bridge. How could they build one when they couldn't reach across? A boat certainly wouldn't get across the rushing water; it would just be pushed over the falls. The answer was to have a contest— a kite-flying contest! A young boy named Homan Walsh was able to sail his kite across Niagara Falls. (He won a prize of five dollars.)

A heavy rope and some cables were tied to the kite string. Then it was pulled back across the falls, dragging the first supplies for the new bridge along with it.

The Niagara waterfall is so powerful that it frightens people. They know that if the water ever washed over them, they couldn't stand up against it. God used the example of rushing water to tell how he wanted us to behave. He said, "I want to see a mighty flood of justice—a torrent of doing good" (Amos 5:24). He wants so many people doing so many good things that the rest of the world won't be able to resist.

66
What trapped
a fire truck?

The firefighters in Stratford, Connecticut, had a big problem that was sort of a mystery. When the alarm sounded and the truck started to roar out of the firehouse, the overhead door would close, blocking the truck from leaving. The firefighters would have to stop, get the door open, and then get going. Obviously, something had to be done.

The people who had installed the door were called to come for an inspection. The mystery was finally solved. The fire truck's radio came on whenever the truck was started. The radio sent a signal that was exactly the same as the one that the garage door opener used. The garage door couldn't tell them apart. So when the truck was turned on, the door went down.

Firefighters have very important jobs, and when a closed door blocks their path, they can't answer a call for help. Whenever you call for Jesus, nothing will stop his coming to you. The Bible says, "Be lifted up, you ancient doors, that the King of glory may come in" (Psalm 24:7, NIV). No gate, door, or lock can stop him. The thing he wants most is to be with you.

What's the good of garlic?

67

Try this strange experiment: Rub a piece of garlic on the bottom of your foot. In just a few minutes, your breath will smell like garlic. How does this happen? The oil in the garlic goes through your skin. It enters your blood, and the blood goes into your lungs. When the air comes out of your lungs through your mouth, so does the strong smell of garlic.

Why would anyone want to use a plant that smells like that? Throughout history, garlic has been used for many jobs. At one time it was rubbed on meat to keep the meat from spoiling. Garlic has also been used as a cure for more than 60 different sicknesses. It was even used to help with snakebites. Garlic was thought to cure the flu. It was boiled in water, and the steam was breathed into the nose to clear up stuffiness. Actually, garlic really did help with many of these situations. It's true that garlic kills germs—even better than some antibiotics, which are the medicines that were invented more recently. Doctors in World War I even wiped garlic into soldier's wounds because it helped keep infection away. But garlic is not just for people—cats and dogs love the taste, and most of their canned food has garlic in it.

God cares so much for us that he created many plants to help us. The Bible says, "He makes grass grow for the cattle, and plants for man to cultivate—bringing forth food from the earth" (Psalm 104:14, NIV). Garlic is just one of the creations God gave to us to make our lives better.

68
How do flies walk on the ceiling?

If you have imagined that a fly has suction cups on its feet, you're getting the wrong picture. A fly that stuck itself to the ceiling with suction wouldn't be able to fly away quickly, which you know a fly can do if you've ever tried to swat one. The truth is that the fly has small claws, like a lobster's, on each of its six legs. These claws can grab the rough surfaces on the ceiling. The fly also has pads, called *pulvilli,* on the end of each leg. These pulvilli are fuzzy and covered with a sticky goo, allowing the fly to stay on metal or glass as well as ceilings.

People don't have the same abilities as flies do to walk on ceilings. But that doesn't mean that God has neglected us. Far from it! God watches over us everywhere we walk. The Bible says, "My steps have held to your paths; my feet have not slipped" (Psalm 17:5, NIV). God gave the fly sticky feet to hold it up. For us, though, God himself holds our feet to make sure that we stick to his paths of safety.

69
Why does aluminum foil have a shiny side and a dull side?

If you're good at noticing things, you may have discovered something curious about aluminum foil—one side is shiny, and the other side is dull. Some people say the shiny side is supposed to be closest to the food. Others think the dull side is supposed to face the food. Who is right? Neither one. It makes no difference when you're cooking. Actually, no one made the two sides different on purpose—it just happens when the foil is made.

Foil starts out as a big block of aluminum. It is flattened with a roller until it is long and thin. Then, two sheets of foil are put through the rollers back-to-back at the same time. The big, heavy rollers are very smooth and shiny, so the sides of the foil that touch the rollers also get smooth and shiny. The sides of the foil that are pressed against each other don't get polished by the rollers, so those sides stay dull.

If you have noticed that the two sides of foil don't look the same, you are an alert person. Jesus wants us to be alert—to be aware of what is going on around us. The more you see, the more you learn. Jesus said, "What I say to you, I say to everyone: 'Watch!'" (Mark 13:37, NIV). Jesus also wants us to watch out for times when we'll be tempted to do something wrong. Being observant about little things, like aluminum foil, is good practice.

70

Why do people say, "I'll eat my hat if I'm wrong"?

Many times, we say words or phrases without really knowing where they came from, why we say them, or what they used to mean. When people say, "If I'm wrong, I'll eat my hat!" they aren't really talking about what sits on their heads.

Long ago, there was a terrible-tasting food made from eggs, dates, and veal. It was called *hattes*. When you were promising to do something, you'd say you absolutely would or "eat hattes" as your punishment. When nobody cooked that dish anymore, people forgot its name but still promised to eat hattes. Eventually people just thought it meant the hats we wear.

It really doesn't matter that people forgot what *hattes* meant, because a dish of food is not very important. You wouldn't want to forget where your house was, though, or that a hot stove can burn your hand. Some things are important, and those are the things we should be sure to remember. The Bible tells us, "Hold tightly to the pattern of truth I taught you, especially concerning the faith and love Christ Jesus offers you" (2 Timothy 1:13). There is nothing more important to remember than that Jesus came to save us. It's so important that

Christians keep saying it over and over, to make sure that no one ever forgets.

71

Who invented Frisbees?

Using a pie plate to play with doesn't sound like much fun, but that's not what the students at Yale University thought. They tossed the plates back and forth to each other on the college grounds after they had bought and eaten the pies baked in the tin plates by the Frisbie Pie Company. To warn people to watch out for the flying pie plate, the students would yell out, "Frisbie!"

The first plastic toy shaped like a pie plate came from Fred Morrison in 1948, but he called it a Pluto Platter. Everyone at that time was excited about outer space, and the plastic disc looked like a flying saucer. But the name didn't work—too many people thought the toy was named after the Disney cartoon character Pluto the dog. The name was finally changed to *Frisbee,* spelled just a little bit differently than the pie company's name.

In the meantime, Mr. Morrison thought of an interesting way to sell his toy. He went to a county fair and rented a booth. Then he walked through the fairgrounds, pretending that he was stringing up a wire, and yelling, "Make way! Make way for the wire!" Mr. Morrison was trying to get people's attention. He told the crowd who gathered around him that he would toss the Frisbee, which would then float magically across the wire to his assistant. That's exactly what the Frisbee appeared to do. Mr. Morrison told the crowd that he would give the Frisbee away for free, but they must buy one hundred yards of the imaginary wire for one cent a yard. Of course, people knew that the wire was just a joke, but they wanted the Frisbee anyway.

The college boys who first started throwing pie plates had no idea that they were inventing such a popular game. They thought they were just having fun. God likes young people to play, as long as they are staying within his rules. The Bible says, "Be happy, young man, while you are young, and let your heart give you joy in the days of your youth" (Ecclesiastes 11:9, NIV). God gives us a childhood to enjoy.

_____ *72*

Which inventions were never used?

People are always trying to come up with better ideas. Some inventions become famous. Some are never heard of again. Here are some ideas that never became popular. See if you can figure out why.

The Chewing Brush: It's a little brush with no handle that you pop into your mouth and chew on. It's for people whose hands are too busy to take the time to hold a regular toothbrush. (Defect—It could be swallowed.)

The Backward/Forward Shoe: The top of the shoe is normal and faces the same direction as your foot does. The sole, or bottom of the shoe, is reversed. The heel is underneath

your toes. Why? Anyone following your footprints will think that you went in the oppo-
site direction than you're really walking. The
shoe makes a backwards footprint each time
you step. (Defect—It won't work on pave-
ment, and not many people would need it in
the first place.)

Spike for the Bike: If someone tries to steal
this bike, it could be an uncomfortable expe-
rience. There is a spike that can be raised or
lowered in the middle of the seat. Raise the
spike when you're away from your bike, and
no one will be tempted to hop on. (Defect—
The bike can just be rolled away.)

The Thumb Twiddler: A small cylinder
with holes on either side for your thumbs.
You rotate your thumbs around and around
in this wheel, and it counts how many times
you've twiddled. (Defect—Who would care
to know?)

The people who thought of these inventions probably spent lots of time on them.
But the things they made weren't very useful. The Bible tells us that if you really want
to use your time wisely, you should "spend
your time and energy in the exercise of

keeping spiritually fit" (1 Timothy 4:7). Read the Bible. Make time to pray. Think of all the blessings that God has given you. Try to do something nice for someone else. These are exercises that will make your faith stronger and make good use of your time.

73

How was exercising turned into a game?

Some toys can actually be good for your health. The Hula Hoop is one of them. Australian kids in 1958 were using a bamboo hoop during exercise time in school. The owners of the Wham-O Toy Company saw these hoops and decided that American kids might enjoy them. So they made some wooden hoops and went out to playgrounds in California to show kids how to twirl them around their waists. Any child who could twirl the hoop got to keep it. Soon everyone wanted to play with this new toy. The toy company thought about calling it the Swing-A-Hoop or the Twirl-A-Hoop, but finally decided on the Hula Hoop, after the Hawaiian dance. They made the hoop out of plastic in bright colors and even added little pellets inside the plastic so the hoop would make a noise as it twirled. One hundred million Hula Hoops were sold in the first two years. That's a lot of exercising!

Circles like the Hula Hoop have no beginning and no end. When you put a Hula Hoop around your waist, there is no way to break through it. That's the way God wants to surround you, too. The Bible says, "Just as the mountains surround and protect Jerusalem, so the Lord surrounds and protects his people" (Psalm 125:2). You do not need to be afraid when God is surrounding you. He will go before you and behind you just like a big Hula Hoop, keeping you from harm.

What's a googol?

Each number has a name—like four, or eighty, or two million. If you were in charge, what name would you pick for a new number? Nine-year-old Milton Sirotta made up a very strange name for a new number.

Milton's uncle was a mathematician, someone who knows a lot about numbers. Milton's uncle said there was a number that was so big that it was hard to understand. Write the number one on paper, and then write 100 zeroes after it. No one had done much thinking about a number that big, so it didn't even have a name. One day, Milton made up a silly name for the number. He called it a *googol,* just for fun. Milton's uncle told the people he worked with what Milton had said, and soon they were calling the number a googol, too. In 1940, Milton's uncle wrote a book about mathematics, and he used the word *googol* in it. Now everyone knows about Milton's silly word, but it isn't considered silly anymore. And just how big is a googol? Milton's uncle said that if we counted every word ever spoken since people first began to talk, all of those words would not be enough to be even one googol.

That's a lot! But even a googol can't measure God's love. "I can't even count how many times a day your thoughts turn toward me. And when I waken in the morning, you are still thinking of me!" (Psalm 139:18). The smartest mathematician with the most powerful computer in the whole world will never be able to think of enough numbers to start counting God's goodness to us. That's how big God is!

75
When was a canteen alive?

If you were going to travel across a desert, and the canteen or Thermos hadn't been invented yet, and there were no gas stations where you could buy juice or soda, how would you keep from getting thirsty? The Pima Indians had a good answer. They carried water inside an old cactus. Not just any cactus would do—it had to be a certain kind of cactus called a *saguaro.*

Strangely enough, the saguaro cactus was the favorite living place for the gila woodpecker. The woodpecker pecked at the cactus until it made a hole big enough for its nest. Then the cactus tried to heal itself by growing a layer of tissue all around the inside of the hole. The tissue looked like cork. Later, the woodpecker left, and the cactus died and rotted away. Left on the ground was the hard shell that the cactus had grown. The Indians picked this container up, filled it with water, and went on their way.

God knows that we get thirsty and must have water to keep living. That is why he made sure that the Indians had a way to carry water with them. Because water is so important to us, the Bible tells us about God by comparing him to water. It says, "Come, all you who are thirsty, come to the waters"

(Isaiah 55:1, NIV). This means that God will always give you what you need most of all.

76
What's it like to be swallowed by a whale?

Once there was a sailor named James Bartley, and what happened to him in 1891 was almost unbelievable. James worked on a whaling ship—chasing whales, harpooning them, and collecting their blubber. One day, one of the men on James's boat threw a harpoon at a whale, and instead of swimming away, the whale attacked the boat by trying to bite it. Every man but James jumped overboard. James waited too long: He was in charge of the boat, and he was hoping he could get the boat out of danger. Instead, he slipped into the mouth of the whale and disappeared.

His shipmates were horrified, and they

decided to wait for a few hours to see if one of the whales they had hit would come back to the surface. Finally, the body of a whale did appear. The men pulled it up next to the boat and began cutting the blubber. When they got to the stomach, they noticed a lump the size of a person. It was James!

They opened the stomach and saw that James was still breathing, so they splashed him with seawater and gave him drinks to wake him up. At first, he was a little confused, but later he remembered sliding down something spongy and landing in a big "sack." It was the whale's stomach. James told of feeling fish there that wriggled away when he touched them. Although it was completely dark, there was just enough air and the whale was just warm enough for James to stay alive.

In the Bible, a man named Jonah was swallowed by a big fish, and later God told the fish to spit Jonah out. Jonah said, "I was locked out of life and imprisoned in the land of death. But, O Lord my God, you have snatched me from the yawning jaws of death!" (Jonah 2:6). God saves many people from danger. If you ask him to, God will make sure that evil doesn't swallow you up. When your heart and your soul belong to God, he will keep you safe.

77
Can a horse count?

Professor Van Osten was excited. His horse, Hans, could count! Over and over, the professor would ask Hans different questions, and Hans would stamp the correct answer with his hoof every time. The professor was sure that Hans could not only count but that he could read and add, too. He must have had the smartest horse in the world!

Finally, another scientist decided to study Hans, to find out what made the horse so smart. By carefully watching the professor, the scientist was able to figure out what was happening. The scientist discovered that Hans couldn't really count on his own. Hans was watching the professor's face whenever a question was asked. The professor didn't mean to, but he changed his expression when Hans had stamped his hoof enough times. The professor was giving away the answer to Hans, just by the way he moved his face. This was proved when the professor stepped behind a screen. Hans was asked a question, but he didn't know the answer because he couldn't see the professor's face. The professor might have been a little sad to know that Hans couldn't add, but Hans was still a very smart horse—he could tell, just by watching his master's face, what he was supposed to do next.

Because we can speak, read, and count, we are smarter than animals. But we are not smarter than God. The Bible says, "Many, O Lord my God, are the wonders you have done. The things you planned for us no one can recount to you; were I to speak and tell of them, they would be too many to declare" (Psalm 40:5, NIV). We could count forever and never be able to add up how many wonderful things God has done. There are not enough words to describe his greatness, even if we use a whole dictionary. And all the paper in the world wouldn't be enough to write down all the ways God is special. God made us the smartest creatures on earth, but he is much, much wiser than we are.

78
What do a tree frog, an ant, and a warthog all have in common?

They all use their heads to protect themselves! There is a tree frog from Mexico called the helmet frog whose head has a bony knob on it. The helmet frog needs to stay wet, and when the weather is too dry, the frog crawls into a hole in a tree and plugs up the hole with its head. The knob on its head becomes the closed door of the hole, and the frog is able to stay moist inside the hole, even during a drought.

There are also ants that live in trees, and

they, too, use their heads as doors. Ants who live there are allowed to go in and out, but stranger ants are stopped when the tree ant closes the hole with its head.

Warthogs, a type of wild hog, also depend on their heads. When they are ready to rest, warthogs back up under some rocks, or into a hole in the ground, or into a cave. Warthogs are prepared to face any danger because they leave their head in the opening. Not only will they be warned if another animal comes, but just seeing the big tusks of the warthog might scare visitors away.

The Bible tells us that we can protect ourselves with our heads, too, but not by poking them into a hole. When we use our heads to think, and to make a decision to follow Jesus Christ, we can wear "the helmet of salvation" (Ephesians 6:17, NIV). A helmet, like the kind you wear when skating or riding a bike, is meant to keep your head from getting injured. Your helmet of salvation will protect your mind from doubting what God has done for you.

79
Is it *catsup* or *ketchup*?

The Chinese invented it with fish and spices; sailors took it to England, where walnuts, cucumbers, and mushrooms were added; and Americans changed the recipe with tomatoes. But no one seems sure how to spell it. Originally, the sauce was called *ketsiap*, which means "pickled fish" in Chinese. Later, the spelling was changed to *kechap*, because that's the way it sounded. Finally, a mistake in printing turned the spelling to *ketchup*, which is the most common way to spell the word now.

Ketchup started in China in the 1600s, went to England in the 1700s, and was first bottled in America in 1876 by a chef whose name you may recognize: Henry Heinz.

Even though people sometimes say and spell ketchup in different ways, it's easy to understand what they mean: They want us to pass the bottle of red sauce. But if people want to get to heaven, the Bible tells us that Jesus is the only way. It says, "There is salvation in no one else! Under all heaven there is no other name for men to call upon to save them" (Acts 4:12). Ask for ketchup, and you'll get a tasty meal. Ask for Jesus, and you'll get forever in heaven.

80
Do you know what to do if you see someone choking?

Long ago, no one really did. It used to be thought that if you pounded the person on the back, it would help—but sometimes that actually makes things worse. The man who figured out the best thing to do was Dr. Harry Heimlich. He was a lung specialist, and he knew that even a choking person probably has some air still in his lungs. Dr. Heimlich tried to think of a way to push the air out of the lungs quickly and forcefully enough to pop out whatever was caught in someone's windpipe. He experimented with lots of ways and finally found one that worked well.

Maybe your mom or dad or one of your teachers knows the "Heimlich maneuver" and can show you how it works. When you're older, you can learn how to do it yourself. If it doesn't work, try it again. Remember—if a person is coughing strongly and is not turning blue, that means he is getting air and probably doesn't need help. But if you see a person who cannot talk, cough, or breathe, he needs emergency help from the Heimlich maneuver.

If you were choking and no one knew what to do, you would be hoping with all your heart that someone would run to Dr. Heimlich and ask him what to do so that you could be saved. Once, some of Jesus' followers, Paul and Silas, were in jail. Their guard realized that his soul was choking because he didn't belong to God. The jailer ran to Paul and Silas in their jail cell, and "he brought them out and begged them, 'Sirs, what must

I do to be saved?' They replied, 'Believe on the Lord Jesus and you will be saved'" (Acts 16:30-31). When your soul is "choking," Jesus can rescue you.

──────────────── *81*
What's the "hobo code"?

During the Great Depression, many Americans had no jobs or money. Men desperate for work rode in the empty cars of trains, going from town to town, hoping to find a better life. When the train stopped, the men, who were often called hobos, would get off and go looking for a meal or a job. When a hobo knocked at the door, many of the townspeople would help by sharing some of their food or paying for a small chore to be done. Other people were mean and unkind. Hobos wanted to share information with the next trainload of men on where they would be welcomed or which places they should avoid. So before getting back on the train, the hobos would leave a secret or hidden message on a fence or wall, describing different addresses. They would leave little drawings that meant, "This man will let you sleep in his shed," or "If you're sick, this doctor will help you," or "Dishonest lady—won't pay you for work." These signals were called the "hobo code," and it was a small way that men who could barely help themselves tried to help others.

If a stranger came to your house asking for help, would your family give it to him? Most of us would quickly pay attention to a man dressed in royal robes or a fancy business suit. But what about a man with a scruffy beard, a tattered shirt, and holes in his shoes? Jesus says, "I tell you the truth, whatever you did for one of the least of these brothers of mine, you did for me" (Matthew 25:40, NIV). God wants us to treat each person we meet as if he were Jesus in disguise. Ask your dad and mom how your family can help someone in need.

82
Why do some people have naturally curly hair?

Have you ever noticed that no matter how hard you try to make your hair look like someone else's, you usually end up looking just like you? That's because God designed your hair especially for you. You were born with tiny holes, called follicles, all over your scalp. Your hair grows out of these holes. If your follicles are round, you have straight hair. Wavy hair comes from oval-shaped follicles, and square follicles make your hair curly. The follicles are so small that you can't see what shape they are. But God knows what shape you have because he picked it out for you. If you try to curl your straight hair and it stays straight anyway, or if you straighten your curly hair, but the curls come bouncing back, don't be upset. The Bible says, "Consider what God has done: Who can straighten what he has made crooked?" (Ecclesiastes 7:13, NIV). God is pleased with his plan for you, so you can be proud of your hair, whatever kind you have. It's part of what makes you special.

83

Why do horses sleep standing up?

A horse likes to sleep on its feet because it's safer: If danger comes, the horse is already standing and can begin to run as soon as it wakes up. Horses also prefer standing because they weigh so much that if they lie down it is sometimes hard for them to breathe. Also, it takes lots of energy for the horse to lie down and get back up. Horses can lock their knees in a standing position, and that's why they don't fall down when they doze off. Something you might see is a mother and colt standing together while they doze. The colt makes sure its whiskers are touching its mother. That way, if she moves, he will know it.

When a horse sees danger, it has to run away to protect itself. But we don't have to depend on our feet or on our speed to help us. In fact, we can stand on the promises of God, and he will protect us. The Bible tells us, "Resist the devil, and *he* will flee from *you*" (James 4:7, NIV, emphasis added). If a horse stands still, he might get attacked. But when you refuse to lie or cheat or steal, the devil has to run away from you! He can't even stay nearby when you refuse to go along with his evil schemes.

84

What kind of food was once sold with a pair of gloves so people could hold it?

It was a long sausage, first invented in Germany. Antoine Feuchtwanger started selling these sausages in America in 1880, but they were so hot, his customers' hands were getting burned. So Antoine gave them each a pair of gloves! Later, he switched to wrapping the sausages in a bread bun.

This sausage had several names. The first name was frankfurter, from the city where the sausage was invented—Frankfurt, Germany. Then the frankfurter got a new name after people noticed that it looked like the long, skinny dog called a dachshund. Then one time a cartoonist drew a picture of the "dachshund sausage" in the newspaper, but he didn't know how to spell *dachshund*. Instead, he just labeled the sausage a "hot dog"—and that's the name that stuck.

Names are a way to describe things and people. The hot dog got its name because of what it looks like. Our names for God describe his importance to us. Jesus said, "You call me 'Master' and 'Lord,' and you do well to say it, for it is true" (John 13:13). What kind of a name would people use to describe you? Would they nickname you "Happy," because you are spreading the joy of belonging to Jesus? Or would you be called "Nosy," because you gossip about others? Think of a nickname for yourself that you would be proud to have, and use it as a reminder of how you want to act.

85
What are some inventions made by kids?

Good ideas don't come just from grown-ups. A fifth-grader named Chris invented a disposable handle for shopping carts. It just snaps onto the cart, and you throw it away when you leave. Why did he make it? So his baby brother could chew on the handle without chewing germs.

Daniel was in kindergarten when he invented the shoe magnet. His shoelaces had metal tips on the ends, and they stuck to magnets on his shoes. That way, even if they came untied, they wouldn't drag on the ground and trip him.

Third-grader Charlie thought of a bowling ball with holes all over it, so bowlers wouldn't have to turn the ball all around looking for the finger holes.

When Alex was in the third grade he figured out a way for just one person to use the seesaw. He made a spring to go beneath the seat, so he could bounce up and down when he was by himself.

Another Daniel, an eighth-grader, invented a safer way for people on crutches to walk on icy sidewalks. He put a cap with sharp spikes over the rubber tip on each crutch. The spikes pierce the ice, and the crutches stay steady.

April noticed that her baby brother cried whenever he had his diaper changed, because their mom used wipes that were too cold. April, who was in third grade, invented an electrical box that heats up the baby wipes.

The Bible says, "Don't let anyone think little of you because you are young. Be their ideal; let them follow the way you teach and live; be a pattern for them in your love, your faith, and your clean thoughts" (1 Timothy 4:12). God wants you to use your mind and heart to make the world a better place. It pleases God when you set a good example and share a good idea.

86
Why was a 107-year-old lady supposed to go to first grade?

Alldora Bjarnadottir was 107 years old, living in Iceland, when she got a letter telling her how much fun she would have when she began going to first grade! Alldora was confused. Who would think that she needed to go back to school?

Finally, the mystery was solved by some people who worked for the government of Iceland. In their country, every child who turned seven needed to start school. The computer that sent out the letters to new first graders could only count people's ages up to 100. After that, it started over. Alldora was 100 plus 7, but the computer thought she was only 7!

Alldora deserved respect for the many years she had lived. The Bible tells us, "White hair is a crown of glory" (Proverbs 16:31). We should listen to older people and respect the wisdom they have gained in their lifetimes. If Alldora was really going back to school, she should go as a teacher rather than a student, because she had already learned 100 years' worth of extra knowledge about life.

How do animals help their friends?

Animals seem to know when a friend is sick, weak, or hurt, and they try to help. Elephants keep a sick relative standing up as long as they can, but if it dies, the elephants cover the body with leaves and dirt, and then stay nearby for several days. Animals that live in water help their sick friends by swimming near them or under them, trying to keep them close to the top of the water so they won't drown. In wild dog families, the dad goes hunting and leaves the mom and cubs behind. When he gets back, he spits the food out of his mouth so the mom and babies can eat it. Sometimes animal families combine, and one healthy grown-up will take care of another family's sick grown-up along with all of the babies from both families.

We can learn a lesson from the animals. The Bible says, "Feed the hungry! Help those in trouble! Then your light will shine out from the darkness, and the darkness around you shall be as bright as day" (Isaiah 58:10). If we do whatever we can to help people who need it, we will be showing the light of God's love. Being kind is a good thing for animals *and* people to do!

88
Why is lemon served with fish?

If you have ordered fish to eat at a restaurant, you may have noticed that a slice of lemon is usually added to your plate with the fish. The cooks and servers may not know it, but they are following a custom that was started way back in history during the Middle Ages. Lemon and fish went together, but not because the lemon was squeezed over the fish to make it taste better. The lemon was served with the fish for safety reasons. In those days, people mistakenly believed that if you swallowed a fish bone, lemon juice would help to dissolve the bone.

It is sad to think that anyone would depend on a lemon to protect them, when we know that the lemon couldn't do any protecting at all. True protection—from swallowing fish bones or any other danger—comes only from God. The Bible tells us, "You bless the godly man, O Lord; you protect him with your shield of love" (Psalm 5:12). Believing in God's power is so much better than believing in the power of a piece of fruit!

89
What unusual tracks did a car leave behind on the road?

There was once a famous movie star named Tom Mix, and he had a very unusual car. It was a fancy Rolls-Royce with a pair of antlers on its hood. The city of Hollywood, where Tom Mix lived, was full of dirt roads at that time, so he had his initials put on the car's tires like a rubber stamp. That way, whenever he drove his car, everyone would know where he had been by following the "TM, TM, TM" tracks that he left printed behind.

What if you had your initials stuck on the bottoms of your shoes, and every time you took a step, they made a stamp showing where you had been? Would your footprints show that you had walked out of your way to help someone pick up a package they had dropped, or would they show that you ran to hide when it was time to help fold the laundry? Would they show that you went to church on Sunday mornings? Would your footprints be found on the sidewalk of your neighbor's house or be tracked through her flower garden because you wanted to take a shortcut? The Bible tells us, "Let everyone see that you are unselfish and considerate in all you do" (Philippians 4:5). Each day, try to do things that are honest and fair and kind, so that if people really could see your initials left behind you, they'd say, "One of God's kids has been here."

90

Why did a brand-new prison fail?

In 1982, a new jail was built in Maryland. It was supposed to be the most modern jail in America, run by computers, and it cost over 11 million dollars to build. But nothing seemed to work like it was supposed to.

There were remote control cameras in the corners, to take pictures of the prisoners at all times—but the cameras could take pictures for only 30 minutes, and then they had to be shut down or the motors would burn up. The locks on most of the doors didn't work. People got stuck where they weren't supposed to be. A sliding door cut off part of a guard's finger. Guards couldn't see the prisoners from their station, and the microphones that they were supposed to use to speak to the prisoners didn't work. The jail was built with solar panels on the roof that were supposed to warm the building. Instead, they froze. Some prisoners escaped by kicking through the glass and plastic windows, which were supposed to be unbreakable.

This story is about a jail made of bricks and glass, but some prisons are not buildings. Your mind can be a prison, because if you think that you will never be successful, your thoughts can hold you back from trying. Your emotions can be a prison. If you stay angry at someone, you are holding yourself back from happiness because you won't forgive. To get help, say to God, "Set me free from my prison, that I may praise your name" (Psalm 142:7, NIV). You won't have to dig or kick or sneak your way out of your prison. God will throw open the door to your heart and mind, and he will free you.

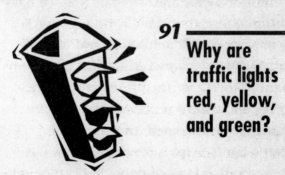

91
Why are traffic lights red, yellow, and green?

The first traffic lights weren't for cars—they were for trains. When railroad signals began to be used in 1830, green meant stop and white meant go. But there were all sorts of problems with the clear, white light. When conductors saw a clear light from far away, they couldn't tell if it was a go light or just a light from a house or street lamp. Also, if the tinted green glass fell out of a stop light, then it looked clear. The train could go rushing ahead, thinking the broken green light was a go instead of a stop. So new colors needed to be picked.

It was easy to pick red for stop. Red is the color of blood, which makes people think of danger. "Go" was changed to green because the color green doesn't have much effect on our emotions. Our brains tell us that we have nothing to fear; that there is no reason to stop or slow down. Yellow became "caution," mainly because yellow is the color that seems brightest when put next to red and green. This system worked much better for trains, so eventually it was copied for cars.

Traffic lights help us to travel safely. But there is another kind of light that can help you much more. This light can give you the power to change your life and overcome

Actual Factuals #1

hardships. If you search for this light, you are guaranteed to find it. The Bible tells us, "The Lord will be my light" (Micah 7:8, NIV). That's right—God is the Light that will brighten your life. You don't even have to travel anywhere to see God's light. He will bring it to you if you just ask.

92

What do gold, tents, a blacksmith, and the country of France have to do with your blue jeans?

Each item played a part in the history of Levi's jeans. Levi Strauss was 17 when he decided to go to California, where there was a big hunt for gold going on called the Gold Rush. Levi was a salesman, so he took his merchandise along on the ship headed to California. He sold all of his goods to the passengers, except for some heavy cloth material. Levi intended to make tents and wagon

157

covers from the cloth, but when he got to San Francisco, the miners told him that what they really wanted were heavy pants that wouldn't tear while they were digging. So Levi had the canvas material sewn into pants, and everyone wanted a pair. The cloth was made in Genoa, Italy, which the French called "Genes." Soon "jeans" became the nickname for the pants.

Later, Levi decided to use a softer material: *serge* (the type of cloth) *de* (from) *Nimes* (the city, pronounced "neem". If you say *serge de Nimes* quickly like the French do, *de Nimes* becomes "denim." Levi decided to dye the pants dark blue because this color made it easier to match pieces for sewing, and it also hid stains.

Cowboys loved the denim jeans. They would jump into a horse-trough full of water and then lie in the sun to shrink the pants to a snug fit.

The rivets, or metal buttons, on the pockets were the idea of a blacksmith named Jacob Davis. Jacob was surprised one day when a man named Alkali brought a pair of Levi's to his blacksmith's shop. Alkali was tired of having his pockets tear when he stuffed rock samples into them. Jacob fixed Alkali's pants by putting rivets on the pockets, and the pockets never tore again. So Levi Strauss went into business with Jacob, and Levi's jeans had rivets on the back pockets until 1932, when they were taken off because teachers complained that the rivets were scratching school desks. Another thing that was special about Levi's jeans was the curved stitching across the back pockets. The only time the stitching was left off was during World War II, when the thread couldn't be wasted just for decoration. (During those years, the curved markings were painted on!)

The story of Levi's is interesting, but if these pants are too expensive for your budget, don't feel badly. The Bible tells us, "Don't worry about *things*—food, drink, and clothes. For you already have life and a body—and they are far more important than what to eat and wear" (Matthew 6:25). If you dress yourself with God's love on the inside, by being kind and caring and generous to others, what you are wearing on the outside won't matter.

_____ 93

Where did the dessert with the wiggle come from?

Jell-O is really gelatin—a gooey, gluey liquid. People have used gelatin for cooking for many years. They used it as a glue to hold foods, like meat, together. It was often flavored with wine, vinegar, or almonds. Gelatin molds used to be very fancy, shaped like fortresses and castles with windows, doors, and notched towers.

Making the gelatin itself often took all day. This gluey gel was only found in the middle of the bones, antlers, knuckles, or feet of animals. To make gelatin, first you had to scrape all the hair off the animal parts. Then you had to boil the gel for hours, then cook it with egg whites to remove the grease. Next, the gel had to be poured through "jelly bags" to let just the smooth part filter through. Finally, the clear gel had to be dried into sheets. What a lot of work! You can imagine how happy people were when they could just add water to a powder to make gelatin in 1890.

Then a lady named May Wait thought of adding sugar and fruit flavors to gelatin. She called her new mix "Jell-O," and she sold the idea to a man named Frank Woodward. To get people to buy Jell-O, Frank had to teach people what to do with it. Frank sent Jell-O salesmen out in fancy buggies, and later cars, to hand out Jell-O recipe books and visit church socials and picnics to show everyone how to make the new dessert.

When you learn of a better way to do something, it can change your mind. Once people saw how easy it was to make Jell-O, they liked it. When Jesus came and told the people how they could be close to God, they said, "Now we have a far better hope, for Christ makes us acceptable to God, and now we may draw near to him"(Hebrews 7:19). Because Jesus told people of a new way to live as God's children, many wanted to follow him. By telling your friends how much Jesus has changed your life, you are giving them a chance to start a better life, too.

94

How can making a mistake make you money?

Sometimes learning from your mistakes can make you rich. That's what happened to Bette Graham. She was a secretary who was a terrible typist. Bette made so many mistakes that the only way she could keep up with fixing them was to have a container of white paint in her desk. Every time she made a mistake, she would brush a little bit of white paint over the wrong letter. The other secretaries liked her idea and asked her to make little paint bottles for them, too.

Bette went to the library and researched how to make a better paint. Before she knew it, Bette was making lots of bottles of what she called "Mistake Out" in her garage, where her son helped her. They used ketchup and mustard bottles full of the new paint to fill smaller containers. Bette decided to name her paint Liquid Paper. Twenty years later, Bette had two hundred people working for her and sold her Liquid Paper business for $47 million.

The mistakes that Bette made were small spelling errors. These mistakes could easily be corrected. But there is one mistake that you don't want to make, because it could affect the rest of your life—and your death. Jesus said, "You are in error because you do not know the Scriptures or the power of God" (Matthew 22:29, NIV). The only way to correct this mistake is to read the Bible. Get to know who God is and what he promises you. Then praise God for all the wonderful things he has done. Thank God for making you able to smell perfume, to taste candy, and to feel a kitten's fur. The biggest bottle of Liquid Paper in the world won't help you as much as knowing God's Word will!

95
What toy was invented specifically to help students study?

A geography teacher named John Spilsbury wanted to find a fun way to help his students remember the map of England. He glued the paper map to a flat piece of wood. Then he took the wood home and cut it into pieces with a small saw called a jigsaw. When the children came to class, they had an interesting assignment. Their job was to learn about England by putting together the first "jigsaw puzzle," which was named after the saw that Mr. Spilsbury used to make it.

If you have ever done a jigsaw puzzle, you know how disappointing it is when one piece is missing and no matter how hard you look for it you cannot find it. Then the picture always has a hole in it. Without Jesus, our lives have a hole in them. But God promises that he will fill our empty place if we ask him to. The Bible says, "'You will seek me and find me when you seek me with all your heart. I will be found by you,' declares the Lord" (Jeremiah 29:13-14, NIV). You will always be able to find Jesus when you look for him.

96
How was a whole country fooled?

The little country of Albania could finally take down their Vacancy sign! The people had been looking for a new leader, and they had asked a prince from another country to come and be their ruler. The prince said yes, and now everyone was waiting for him to arrive.

Finally, a fancy carriage drove into the city, and a tall, thin man got out and said, "Make way for the new prince!" Then a strong-looking man got out. And after him came the prince. The prince made a speech and announced that Albania would now have a whole week of celebrating. Everyone thought this was a great idea.

But one day, a mysterious letter was sent to Albania. It said, "Thank you for asking me to be your prince. Someone told me that you think I am already there. Of course, that is ridiculous. I will be coming soon." The people asked each other, "Then who is the man who came in the coach?" They went to the palace, but he and his two friends were already gone. Later it was discovered that the false prince was really a circus performer and that his two helpers were really the strong man and the giant from the circus.

Sometimes it's easy to be fooled by people. The way they speak and act may be very convincing. But the Bible tells us, "Watch out for false prophets. They come to you in sheep's clothing, but inwardly they are ferocious wolves" (Matthew 7:15, NIV). We should not believe any person who claims to be as good as Jesus. People who try to make you admire them (or something else) more than Jesus may seem nice and gentle like sheep, but they are really mean—like wolves. Stay close to Jesus, and you won't be fooled.

97
What job could you do if you couldn't hear or speak?

Imagine that you couldn't hear or speak. Maybe you would feel that you couldn't do anything else, either. Maybe you would feel sorry for yourself.

Once there was a young man named Leroy Columbo who was not able to hear or speak. But Leroy found something useful to do. Because Leroy depended on his eyes to show him what he couldn't hear, he always watched everything very carefully. Since Leroy's eyes became especially good from all that practice, he decided to become a lifeguard at Galveston Beach in Texas. He sat on the shore every day for 57 years, searching the ocean for swimmers in trouble. Was Leroy good at his job? The people of Galveston thought so. They put a sign on the beach thanking Leroy for saving 907 people from drowning.

The Bible tells us, "Each of you must bring a gift in proportion to the way the Lord your God has blessed you" (Deuteronomy 16:17, NIV). That means God has made sure everyone has something they can do well. He doesn't want us to get upset about what we *can't* do. Instead, God wants us to find our best ability and use it the best way, just like Leroy did.

98

Why did a school put a traffic light in its lunchroom?

If you find that your ears are getting more of a workout than your mouth when you eat lunch in the school cafeteria, you might want to suggest an idea that worked in 1982. In a Tennessee elementary school, something was added to the cafeteria that had never been in there before. It was a traffic light. It was hooked up to a machine that measured sound levels. When the talking was normal, the light stayed green, and the kids knew that they were doing a good job. Louder talking turned the light yellow, and everyone knew they were being warned. If the talking was way too loud, the light turned red. When the red light was on, no one was allowed to talk at all until it turned green again.

It's natural for people to want to talk. That's the way we explain to others how we think and feel. When we're not allowed to talk, it is harder to communicate. Imagine how special it would be if you could just think something and your friend knew exactly what you were thinking without your having to say a word. The Bible reminds us that we do have a Friend like that: "Remember, your Father knows exactly what you need even before you ask him!" (Matthew 6:8). You will always have a green light when you are praying, because God always wants you to talk to him!

99
What letter is used most often in the English language?

It's the letter *e*. We use it all the time to help spell what we want to say.

One man did something very hard. He wrote a whole book without ever using the letter *e*. His name was Earnest Wright, and he spent 165 days writing his book. The book was almost 300 pages long, and it used about 50,000 words. He had to tape down the letter *e* on his typewriter so he would remember not to use it.

Books that leave out a letter have a name of their own—they're called *lipograms*. Just to give yourself a challenge sometime, try this: Pick out a vowel. Make up a sentence. Then search each word of your sentence to see how many times the vowel is there. Now try to make up a new sentence without ever using that vowel. This is a fun game to play.

Maybe someday you'll even write a lipogram of your own!

Lipograms are interesting books, but they are not very useful. They are more like games than places to find information. If you're looking for a book that has something very important to say—something that will change the rest of your life—try the Bible. "The whole Bible was given to us by inspiration from God and is useful to teach us what is true and to make us realize what is wrong in our lives; it straightens us out and helps us do what is right" (2 Timothy 3:16). Every lipogram leaves something out, but the Bible tells you everything you need to know about being God's child.

100
Why wouldn't a locksmith give anyone his key?

Joseph Bramah loved to invent things. He especially liked making locks, and in 1784 he created a lock that he was sure no one could open. He even printed a challenge on the front of the lock, saying that he would pay a reward to anyone who could figure out how to open it without a key. For 60 years, no one was able to collect the money. Three years after Joseph died, someone spent a whole week trying to get the lock open but had to give up. In 1851 there was a big fair in London, and a locksmith named Alfred Hobbs decided he would work on the lock in front of everyone. Alfred spent a few hours every day tinkering with the lock. He had to use many tools, but finally, after a whole month, he opened the lock.

Sometimes people's hearts have locks on them, and they don't want to hear about God. But the Bible tells us that God can open people's hearts and minds. It says, "What he opens no one can shut, and what he shuts no one can open" (Revelation 3:7, NIV). So don't be discouraged if you talk about Jesus and your friend doesn't want to listen. God can use your words as a key to open your friend's closed heart, even if your friend is trying hard to keep it shut.

BIBLIOGRAPHY

1. Why were the police called to an exercise class?
Sobol, Donald and Rose. *Encyclopedia Brown's Book of Strange But True Crimes*. New York: Scholastic, 1992.

2. Which country has a pancake party every year?
Nussbaum, Hedda, ed. *Charlie Brown's Fifth Super Book of Questions and Answers*. New York: Random House, 1981.
Martinet, Jeanne. *The Year You Were Born: A Day-to-Day Record of 1984*. New York: Tambourine Books, 1992.

3. Why does a contest usually have first, second, and third place winners?
Smith, Douglas B. *Ever Wonder Why?* New York: Fawcett Gold Medal, 1992.

4. When was a sunny day bad for baseball?
Goldberg, M. Hirsh. *The Blunder Book*. New York: William Morrow and Co., 1984.

5. Which fish takes aim at its lunch?
Simon, Seymour. *Animal Fact/Animal Fable*. New York: Crown Publishers, 1979.

6. What did people do about their cuts before Band-Aids?
Buchman, Dian Dincin, and Seli Groves. *What If? Fifty Discoveries That Changed the World*. New York: Scholastic, 1988.
Caney, Steven. *Steven Caney's Invention Book*. New York: Workman Publishing, 1985.
Felder, Deborah G. *The Kids' World Almanac of History*. New York: Pharos Books, 1991.
Garrison, Webb. *Why Didn't I Think of That? From Alarm Clocks to Zippers*. Englewood Cliffs, N. J.: Prentice Hall, 1977.
Harris, Harry. *Good Old-Fashioned Yankee Ingenuity*. Chelsea, Mich.: Scarborough House, 1990.

McKenzie, E. C. *Salted Peanuts: 1800 Little-Known Facts*. Grand Rapids, Mich.: Baker Book House, 1972.

McLoone-Basta, Margo, and Alice Siegel. *The Kids' World Almanac of Records and Facts*. New York: World Almanac Publications, 1985.

Polley, Jane, ed. *Stories behind Everyday Things*. New York: Reader's Digest Assn., 1980.

7. How did a little girl's letter change history?

McLoone-Basta, Margo, and Alice Siegel. *The Second Kids' World Almanac of Records and Facts*. New York: World Almanac Publications, 1987.

Thompson, C. E. *101 Wacky Facts about Kids*. New York: Scholastic, 1992.

Varasdi, J. Allen. *Myth Information*. New York: Ballantine Books, 1989.

8. Why are barns red?

Johnny Wonder Question and Answer Book. New York: Playmore, 1984.

Smith, Douglas B. *Ever Wonder Why?* New York: Fawcett Gold Medal, 1992.

9. Which sport started with a fruit basket?

Blumberg, Rhoda and Leda. *The Simon and Schuster Book of Facts and Fallacies*. New York: Simon and Schuster, 1983.

Caney, Steven. *Steven Caney's Invention Book*. New York: Workman Publishing, 1985.

King, Norman. *The Almanac of Fascinating Beginnings*. New York: Citadel Press, 1994.

Smith, Don. *How Sports Began*. New York: Franklin Watts, 1977.

Varasdi, J. Allen. *Myth Information*. New York: Ballantine Books, 1989.

Zotti, Ed. *Know It All!* New York: Ballantine Books, 1993.

10. When did an umbrella make people laugh?

Buchman, Dian Dincin, and Seli Groves. *What If? Fifty Discoveries That Changed the World*. New York: Scholastic, 1988.

Felder, Deborah H. *The Kids' World Almanac of History*. New York: Pharos Books, 1991.

Gray, Ralph, ed. *Small Inventions That Make a Big Difference.*
  Washington, D.C.: The National Geographic Society, 1984.
Meyers, James. *Amazing Facts.* New York: Playmore, 1986.
Meyers, James. *Eggplants, Elevators, Etc.: An Uncommon History
  of Common Things.* New York: Hart Publishing Co., 1978.
Robertson, Patrick. *The Book of Firsts.* New York: Bramhall
  House, 1974.

11. Which president had a giant bathtub?

Asimov, Isaac. *Would You Believe?* New York: Grosset and
  Dunlap, 1982.
McKenzie, E. C. *Salted Peanuts: 1800 Little-Known Facts.* Grand
  Rapids, Mich.: Baker Book House, 1972.
Meyers, James. *Eggplants, Elevators, Etc.: An Uncommon History
  of Common Things.* New York: Hart Publishing Co., 1978.
Sloane, Eric. *ABC Book of Early Americana.* New York: Henry
  Holt and Co., 1963.

12. Can you tell what a bird eats by looking at it?

Blumberg, Rhoda and Leda. *The Simon and Schuster Book of
  Facts and Fallacies.* New York: Simon and Schuster, 1983.
Nussbaum, Hedda, ed. *Charlie Brown's Fifth Super Book of Ques-
  tions and Answers.* New York: Random House, 1981.

13. How was the toothbrush invented?

Felder, Deborah H. *The Kids' World Almanac of History.* New
  York: Pharos Books, 1991.
McLoone-Basta, Margo, and Alice Siegel. *The Kids' World Alma-
  nac of Records and Facts.* New York: World Almanac Publica-
  tions, 1985.
Owl Magazine, eds. *The Kids' Question and Answer Book Two.*
  New York: Grosset and Dunlap, 1988.
Wulffson, Don L. *Extraordinary Stories behind the Invention of
  Ordinary Things.* New York: Lothrop, Lee, and Shepard
  Books, 1981.

14. What makes Mexican jumping beans jump?

Blumberg, Rhoda and Leda. *The Simon and Schuster Book of
  Facts and Fallacies.* New York: Simon and Schuster, 1983.
Goldwyn, Martin M. *How a Fly Walks Upside Down . . . and
  Other Curious Facts.* New York: Citadel Press, 1979.

Manchester, Richard B. *Incredible Facts*. New York: Galahad
Books, 1985.

**15. What did a president of the United States, a
candy seller, and a stuffed animal have to do with a
favorite children's toy?**

Asakawa, Gil, and Leland Rucker. *The Toy Book*. New York:
Alfred A. Knopf, 1992.

Harris, Harry. *Good Old-Fashioned Yankee Ingenuity*. Chelsea,
Mich.: Scarborough House, 1990.

Sanders, Deidre, ed., et al. *Would You Believe This, Too?* New
York: Sterling Publishing Co., 1976.

**16. Why do farmers want their calves to swallow
magnets?**

Chrystie, Frances N. *The First Book of Surprising Facts*. New
York: Franklin Watts, 1956.

Louis, David. *2201 Fascinating Facts*. New York: Greenwich
House Crown Publishers, 1983.

**17. Can a beaver make a tree fall in just the right
spot?**

Blumberg, Rhoda and Leda. *The Simon and Schuster Book of
Facts and Fallacies*. New York: Simon and Schuster, 1983.

Burnam, Tom. *The Dictionary of Misinformation*. New York:
Thomas Y. Crowell Co., 1975.

Fison, Annette, and Falus Taylor. *The Big Book of Amazing Animal Behavior*. New York: Grosset and Dunlap, 1986.

Owl Magazine, eds. *The Kids' Question and Answer Book Three*.
New York: Grosset and Dunlap, 1990.

Rosenbloom, Joseph. *Bananas Don't Grow on Trees: A Guide to
Popular Misconceptions*. New York: Sterling Publishing Co.,
1978.

18. Why keep a broken bell?

Giblin, James Cross. *Fireworks, Picnics, and Flags: The Story of
Fourth of July Symbols*. New York: Houghton Mifflin Co.,
1983.

Wallace, Amy and Irving, and David Wallechinsky. *Significa*.
New York: E. P. Dutton, 1983.

19. Why would anyone be accused of stealing their own car?

Sobol, Donald J. *Encyclopedia Brown's Book of Wacky Cars*. New York: William Morrow and Co., 1987.

20. Why would a bird need goggles?

Johnny Wonder Question and Answer Book. New York: Playmore, 1984.

21. Why did a dog want to live in a graveyard?

Asimov, Isaac. *Would You Believe?* New York: Grosset and Dunlap, 1982.

Wallace, Amy and Irving, and David Wallechinsky. *Significa*. New York: E. P. Dutton, 1983.

22. Why did a cookbook include a recipe for an explosion?

Goldberg, M. Hirsh. *The Blunder Book*. New York: William Morrow and Co., 1984.

23. Can someone be double-jointed?

Blumberg, Rhoda and Leda. *The Simon and Schuster Book of Facts and Fallacies*. New York: Simon and Schuster, 1983.

Gottlieb, William P. *Science Facts You Won't Believe*. New York: Franklin Watts, 1983.

24. How can you read when you can't even see?

Buchman, Dian Dincin, and Seli Groves. *What If? Fifty Discoveries That Changed the World*. New York: Scholastic, 1988.

Gray, Ralph, ed. *Small Inventions That Make a Big Difference*. Washington, D.C.: The National Geographic Society, 1984.

McLoone-Basta, Margo, and Alice Siegel. *The Second Kids' World Almanac of Records and Facts*. New York: World Almanac Publications, 1987.

———. *The Kids' World Almanac of Records and Facts*. New York: World Almanac Publications, 1985.

25. When do parents want their kids to make noise?

Elwood, Ann, and Carol Orsag. *Macmillan Illustrated Almanac for Kids*. New York: Macmillan Publishing Co., 1981.

26. How could the idea of bungee jumping be over 100 years old?

De Vries, Leonard. *Victorian Inventions*. New York: American Heritage Press, 1971.

Murphy, Jim. *Guess Again: More Weird and Wacky Inventions*. New York: Bradbury Press, 1986.

27. If you burn your hand, what is the best thing to do?

Simon, Seymour. *Body Sense, Body Nonsense*. New York: J. B. Lippincott, 1981.

28. How did electricity surprise a whole crowd?

De Vries, Leonard. *Victorian Inventions*. New York: American Heritage Press, 1971.

29. Why do boys' and girls' shirts button on different sides?

Panati, Charles. *Panati's Extraordinary Origins of Everyday Things*. New York: Harper and Row, 1987.

Smith, Douglas B. *Ever Wonder Why?* New York: Fawcett Gold Medal, 1992.

30. Why were M&M's invented?

Choron, Sandra. *The Big Book of Kids' Lists*. New York: World Almanac Publications, 1985.

Felder, Deborah H. *The Kids' World Almanac of History*. New York: Pharos Books, 1991.

Harris, Harry. *Good Old-Fashioned Yankee Ingenuity*. Chelsea, Mich.: Scarborough House, 1990.

King, Norman. *The Almanac of Fascinating Beginnings*. New York: Citadel Press, 1994.

Louis, David. *2201 Fascinating Facts*. New York: Greenwich House Crown Publishers, 1983.

McLoone-Basta, Margo, and Alice Siegel. *The Kids' World Almanac of Records and Facts*. New York: World Almanac Publications, 1985.

Varasdi, J. Allen. *Myth Information*. New York: Ballantine Books, 1989.

31. How can you move an elephant?

Lurie, Susan, ed. *The Big Book of Amazing Knowledge*. New York: Playmore, 1987.

32. How did a toy stop an army?

Wallace, Amy and Irving, and David Wallechinsky. *Significa.* New York: E. P. Dutton, 1983.

33. How did the propeller of a ship help invent the cash register?

Buchman, Dian, and Seli Groves. *What If? Fifty Discoveries That Changed the World.* New York: Scholastic, 1988.

Gray, Ralph, ed. *Small Inventions That Make a Big Difference.* Washington, D.C.: The National Geographic Society, 1984.

Harris, Harry. *Good Old-Fashioned Yankee Ingenuity.* Chelsea, Mich.: Scarborough House, 1990.

Robertson, Patrick. *The Book of Firsts.* New York: Bramhall House, 1974.

Smith, Douglas B. *Ever Wonder Why?* New York: Fawcett Gold Medal, 1992.

34. What haven't you noticed when watching the clock?

Leokum, Arkady. *The Curious Book.* New York: Sterling Publishing Co., 1976.

Zotti, Ed. *Know It All!* New York: Ballantine Books, 1993.

35. Why does a cat lick like that?

Squire, Ann. *101 Questions and Answers about Pets and People.* New York: Macmillan Publishing Co., 1988.

36. When did a softball player catch a flying baby?

Wulffson, Don L. *Amazing True Stories.* New York: Scholastic, 1991.

37. Since fish are always in schools, aren't they smart?

Achenbach, Joel. *Why Things Are: Answers to Every Essential Question in Life.* New York: Ballantine Books, 1991.

38. How did the cavemen build their caves?

Goldwyn, Martin M. *How a Fly Walks Upside Down . . . and Other Curious Facts.* New York: Citadel Press, 1979.

Nussbaum, Hedda, ed. *Charlie Brown's Fifth Super Book of Questions and Answers.* New York: Random House, 1981.

39. Why do chickens wear contact lenses?

Sobol, Donald J. *Encyclopedia Brown's Second Record Book of Weird and Wonderful Facts.* New York: Delacorte Press, 1981.

40. If someone told you to be quiet, would you never speak again?

Manchester, Richard B. *Incredible Facts.* New York: Galahad Books, 1985.

41. How did chop suey get its name?

Harris, Harry. *Good Old-Fashioned Yankee Ingenuity.* Chelsea, Mich.: Scarborough House, 1990.

Louis, David. *2201 Fascinating Facts.* New York: Greenwich House Crown Publishers, 1983.

Perko, Marko. *Did You Know That . . . ?* New York: Berkley Books, 1994.

Rovin, Jeff. *The Unbelievable Truth!* New York: Penguin Books, 1994.

Varasdi, J. Allen. *Myth Information.* New York: Ballantine Books, 1989.

Vogel, Malvina G., ed. *The Big Book of Amazing Facts.* New York: Playmore, 1980.

42. Why did Cinderella wear glass slippers?

Goldberg, M. Hirsh. *The Blunder Book.* New York: William Morrow and Co., 1984.

Jones, Charlotte Foltz. *Mistakes That Worked.* New York: Doubleday, 1991.

Varasdi, J. Allen. *Myth Information.* New York: Ballantine Books, 1989.

43. What made feeding babies more fun?

Aaseng, Nathan. *The Problem Solvers.* Minneapolis: Lerner Publications Co., 1989.

Burnam, Tom. *More Misinformation.* New York: Ballantine Books, 1989.

Harris, Harry. *Good Old-Fashioned Yankee Ingenuity.* Chelsea, Mich.: Scarborough House, 1990.

44. How did people wake up on time before alarm clocks?

Lurie, Susan, ed. *The Big Book of Amazing Knowledge.* New York: Playmore, 1987.

Murphy, Jim. *Weird and Wacky Inventions*. New York: Crown
  Publishers, 1978.
Reader's Digest Facts and Fallacies. New York: The Reader's
  Digest Assn., 1988.

45. How can you tell where a coin was made?

Louis, David. *2201 Fascinating Facts*. New York: Greenwich
  House Crown Publishers, 1983.
Smith, Douglas B. *Ever Wonder Why?* New York: Fawcett Gold
  Medal, 1992.
Sobol, Donald J. *Encyclopedia Brown's Second Record Book of
  Weird and Wonderful Facts*. New York: Delacorte Press, 1981.
Vogel, Malvina G., ed. *The Big Book of Amazing Facts*. New
  York: Playmore, 1980.

46. Why aren't there more green flowers?

Ardley, Bridget and Neil. *The Random House Book of 1001 Ques-
  tions and Answers*. New York: Random House, 1989.
Owl Magazine, eds. *The Kids' Question and Answer Book Two*.
  New York: Grosset and Dunlap, 1988.

47. Are you feeling red, pink, or yellow today?

Aylward, Jim. *Your Burro Is No Jackass!* New York: Holt, Rine-
  hart and Winston, 1981.
Simon, Seymour. *Body Sense, Body Nonsense*. New York: J. B.
  Lippincott, 1981.
Sobol, Donald J. *Encyclopedia Brown's Third Record Book of
  Weird and Wonderful Facts*. New York: William Morrow and
  Co., 1985.

48. What bird gives its babies up for adoption?

Cobb, Vicki. *Why Doesn't The Earth Fall Up?* New York: E. P.
  Dutton, 1988.

49. Why do golfers yell *fore?*

Smith, Douglas B. *Ever Wonder Why?* New York: Fawcett Gold
  Medal, 1992.

50. What happens when you grab a crab?

Blumberg, Rhoda and Leda. *The Simon and Schuster Book of
  Facts and Fallacies*. New York: Simon and Schuster, 1983.

Nussbaum, Hedda, ed. *Charlie Brown's Fifth Super Book of Questions and Answers.* New York: Random House, 1981.

Rosenbloom, Joseph. *Polar Bears Like It Hot.* New York: Sterling Publishing Co., 1980.

51. What's the fastest-growing plant in the world?

Harvey, Edmund, ed. *Reader's Digest Book of Facts.* New York: Reader's Digest Assn., 1987.

52. How did frogs fall from the sky?

Branley, Franklyn M. *It's Raining Cats and Dogs: All Kinds of Weather and Why We Have It.* Boston: Houghton Mifflin Co., 1987.

53. Why would a man be glad to live in a cabinet?

Wallace, Amy and Irving, and David Wallechinsky. *Significa.* New York: E. P. Dutton, 1983.

54. Did George Washington really have wooden teeth?

Felton, Bruce. *One of a Kind.* New York: William Morrow and Co., 1992.

Gray, Ralph, ed. *Small Inventions That Make a Big Difference.* Washington, D.C.: The National Geographic Society, 1984.

55. Why do we call it the "funny bone" when it definitely isn't?

Blumberg, Rhoda and Leda. *The Simon and Schuster Book of Facts and Fallacies.* New York: Simon and Schuster, 1983.

Owl Magazine Editors. *The Kids' Question and Answer Book Three.* New York: Grosset and Dunlap, 1990.

Smith, Douglas B. *Ever Wonder Why?* New York: Fawcett Gold Medal, 1992.

Varasdi, J. Allen. *Myth Information.* New York: Ballantine Books, 1989.

56. Which dogs were asked to dinner?

Manchester, Richard B. *Incredible Facts.* New York: Galahad Books, 1985.

57. Did you know that you've probably used a cup named after a doll factory?

Campbell, Hannah. *Why Did They Name It . . . ?* New York: Ace Books, 1964.

Caney, Steven. *Steven Caney's Invention Book.* New York: Workman Publishing, 1985.

Garrison, Webb. *Why Didn't I Think of That? From Alarm Clocks to Zippers.* New Jersey: Prentice Hall, 1977.

King, Norman. *The Almanac of Fascinating Beginnings.* New York: Citadel Press, 1994.

58. If a marble and a bowling ball raced down a ramp, which one would win?

Cobb, Vicki. *Why Doesn't the Earth Fall Up?* New York: E. P. Dutton, 1988.

59. Who had the biggest dollhouse ever?

Glubok, Shirley. *Dolls' Houses: Life in Miniature.* U.S.A.: Harper and Row Publishers, 1984.

Jacobs, Flora Gill. *A World of Doll Houses.* New York: Gramercy Publishing Co., 1965.

Polley, Jane, ed. *Stories Behind Everyday Things.* New York: Reader's Digest Assn., 1980.

60. When did a dog deliver mail?

Wallace, Amy and Irving, and David Wallechinsky. *Significa.* New York: E. P. Dutton, 1983.

61. Why do giraffes have such long necks?

Ardley, Neil, et. al. *Why Things Are.* New York: Simon and Schuster, 1984.

McGrath, Susan. *The Amazing Things That Animals Do.* Washington, D.C.: The National Geographic Society, 1989.

62. How was a sinking ship saved by a comic book?

Wallace, Amy and Irving, and David Wallechinsky. *Significa.* E. P. Dutton, 1983.

63. Who was Chester Greenwood, and why did he cover his ears?

Caney, Steven. *Steven Caney's Invention Book*. New York: Workman Publishing, 1985.

Gray, Ralph, ed. *Small Inventions That Make a Big Difference*. Washington, D.C.: The National Geographic Society, 1984.

Harris, Harry. *Good Old-Fashioned Yankee Ingenuity*. Chelsea, Mich.: Scarborough House, 1990.

McKenzie, E. C. *Salted Peanuts: 1800 Little-Known Facts*. Grand Rapids, Mich.: Baker Book House, 1972.

McLoone-Basta, Margo, and Alice Siegel. *The Second Kids' World Almanac of Records and Facts*. New York: World Almanac Publications, 1987.

64. When does a board game take a test?

Asakawa, Gil, and Leland Rucker. *The Toy Book*. New York: Alfred A. Knopf, 1992.

65. How did they build a bridge across Niagara Falls?

Hicks, Donna E. *The Most Fascinating Places on Earth*. New York: Sterling Publishing Co., 1993.

66. What trapped a fire truck?

Sobol, Donald J. *Encyclopedia Brown's Second Record Book of Weird and Wonderful Facts*. New York: Delacorte Press, 1981.

67. What's the good of garlic?

Morris, Scot. *The Emperor Who Ate the Bible and More Strange Facts and Useless Information*. New York: Doubleday, 1991.

Robbins, Pat, ed. *More Far-Out Facts*. Washington, D.C.: The National Geographic Society, 1982.

68. How do flies walk on the ceiling?

Burnam, Tom. *More Misinformation*. New York: Ballantine Books, 1980.

Goldwyn, Martin M. *How a Fly Walks Upside Down . . . and Other Curious Facts*. New York: Citadel Press, 1979.

Perko, Marko. *Did You Know That . . . ?* New York: Berkley Books, 1994.

Varasdi, J. Allen. *Myth Information*. New York: Ballantine Books, 1989.

Vogel, Malvina G., ed. *The Big Book of Amazing Facts*. New York: Playmore, 1980.

69. Why does aluminum foil have a shiny side and a dull side?

Feldman, David. *Why Do Clocks Run Clockwise? and Other Imponderables*. New York: Harper and Row, 1987.

70. Why do people say, "I'll eat my hat if I'm wrong"?

Smith, Douglas B. *Ever Wonder Why?* New York: Fawcett Gold Medal, 1992.

71. Who invented Frisbees?

Asakawa, Gil, and Leland Rucker. *The Toy Book*. New York: Alfred A. Knopf, 1992.

Caney, Steven. *Steven Caney's Invention Book*. New York: Workman Publishing, 1985.

Elwood, Ann, and Carol Orsag. *Macmillan Illustrated Almanac for Kids*. New York: Macmillan Publishing Co., 1981.

Felder, Deborah H. *The Kids' World Almanac of History*. New York: Pharos Books, 1991.

Harris, Harry. *Good Old-Fashioned Yankee Ingenuity*. Chelsea, Mich.: Scarborough House, 1990.

Johnny Wonder Question and Answer Book. New York: Playmore, 1984.

Jones, Charlotte Foltz. *Mistakes That Worked*. New York: Doubleday, 1991.

King, Norman. *The Almanac of Fascinating Beginnings*. New York: Citadel Press, 1994.

McLoone-Basta, Margo, and Alice Siegel. *The Second Kids' World Almanac of Records and Facts*. New York: World Almanac Publications, 1987.

Rovin, Jeff. *The Unbelievable Truth!* New York: Penguin Books, 1994.

72. Which inventions were never used?

Editors of Time-Life Books. *Inventive Genius*. Alexandria, Va.: Time-Life, 1991.

73. How was exercising turned into a game?

Asakawa, Gil, and Leland Rucker. *The Toy Book*. New York: Alfred A. Knopf, 1992.

Harris, Harry. *Good Old-Fashioned Yankee Ingenuity.* Chelsea, Mich.: Scarborough House, 1990.

Panati, Charles. *Panati's Parade of Fads, Follies, and Manias.* New York: HarperCollins, 1991.

74. What's a googol?

Elwood, Ann, and Carol Orsag. *Macmillan Illustrated Almanac for Kids.* New York: Macmillan Publishing Co., 1981.

Louis, David. *2201 Fascinating Facts.* New York: Greenwich House Crown Publishers, 1983.

Vogel, Malvina G., ed. *The Big Book of Amazing Facts.* New York: Playmore, 1980.

Wallace, Amy and Irving, and David Wallechinsky. *Significa.* New York: E. P. Dutton, 1983.

75. When was a canteen alive?

Harvey, Edmund, ed. *Reader's Digest Book of Facts.* New York: Reader's Digest Assn., 1987.

76. What's it like to be swallowed by a whale?

McCormick, Donald. *The Master Book of Escapes.* New York: Franklin Watts, 1975.

Tallarico, Tony. *I Didn't Know That! about Strange But True Mysteries.* Illinois: Kidsbooks, 1992.

Wallace, Amy and Irving, and David Wallechinsky. *Significa.* New York: E. P. Dutton, 1983.

77. Can a horse count?

Fison, Annette, and Falus Taylor. *The Big Book of Amazing Animal Behavior.* New York: Grosset and Dunlap, 1986.

78. What do a tree frog, an ant, and a warthog all have in common?

Feldman, Eve B. *Animals Don't Wear Pajamas: A Book about Sleeping.* New York: Henry Holt, 1992.

Harvey, Edmund, ed. *Reader's Digest Book of Facts.* New York: Reader's Digest Assn., Inc, 1987.

79. Is it *catsup* or *ketchup*?

Felder, Deborah H. *The Kids' World Almanac of History.* New York: Pharos Books, 1991.

Feldman, David. *Who Put the Butter in Butterfly?* New York: Harper and Row, 1989.

McLoone-Basta, Margo, and Alice Siegel. *The Kids' World Almanac of Records and Facts.* New York: World Almanac Publications, 1985.

80. Do you know what to do if you see someone choking?

Buchman, Dian Dincin, and Seli Groves. *What If? Fifty Discoveries That Changed the World.* New York: Scholastic, 1988.

Kunz, Jeffery R. M., ed. *Family Medical Guide.* New York: Random House, 1982.

81. What's the "hobo code"?

Mulvey, Deb, ed. *We Had Everything But Money.* Greendale, Wis.: Reiman Publications, 1992.

82. Why do some people have naturally curly hair?

Ardley, Bridget and Neil. *The Random House Book of 1001 Questions and Answers.* New York: Random House, 1989.

Elwood, Ann, and Carol Orsag. *Macmillan Illustrated Almanac for Kids.* New York: Macmillan Publishing Co., 1981.

Goldwyn, Martin M. *How a Fly Walks Upside Down . . . and Other Curious Facts.* New York: Citadel Press, 1979.

Vogel, Malvina G., ed. *The Big Book of Amazing Facts.* New York: Playmore, 1980.

83. Why do horses sleep standing up?

Blumberg, Rhoda and Leda. *The Simon and Schuster Book of Facts and Fallacies.* New York: Simon and Schuster, 1983.

Chrystie, Frances N. *The First Book of Surprising Facts.* New York: Franklin Watts, 1956.

Louis, David. *2201 Fascinating Facts.* New York: Greenwich House Crown Publishers, 1983.

Squire, Ann. *101 Questions and Answers about Pets and People.* New York: Macmillan Publishing Co., 1988.

Zotti, Ed. *Know It All!* New York: Ballantine Books, 1993.

84. What kind of food was once sold with a pair of gloves so people could hold it?

Felder, Deborah H. *The Kids' World Almanac of History.* New York: Pharos Books, 1991.

McLoone-Basta, Margo, and Alice Siegel. *The Kids' World Almanac of Records and Facts*. New York: World Almanac Publications, 1985.

Morris, Scot. *The Emperor Who Ate the Bible and More Strange Facts and Useless Information*. New York: Doubleday, 1991.

Smith, Douglas B. *Ever Wonder Why?* New York: Fawcett Gold Medal, 1992.

Sutton, Caroline. *How Did They Do That?* New York: William Morrow and Co., 1984.

85. What are some inventions made by kids?

Taylor, Barbara. *Be an Inventor*. Florida: Harcourt Brace Jovanovich, 1987.

86. Why was a 107-year-old lady supposed to go to first grade?

Sobol, Donald J. *Encyclopedia Brown's Third Record Book of Weird and Wonderful Facts*. New York: William Morrow and Co., 1985.

87. How do animals help their friends?

Fison, Annette, and Falus Taylor. *The Big Book of Amazing Animal Behavior*. New York: Grosset and Dunlap, 1986.

88. Why is lemon served with fish?

Louis, David. *2201 Fascinating Facts*. New York: Greenwich House Crown Publishers, 1983.

Rovin, Jeff. *The Unbelievable Truth!* New York: Penguin Books, 1994.

89. What unusual tracks did a car leave behind on the road?

Louis, David. *2201 Fascinating Facts*. New York: Greenwich House Crown Publishers, 1983.

90. Why did a brand-new prison fail?

Goldberg, M. Hirsh. *The Blunder Book*. New York: William Morrow and Co., 1984.

91. Why are traffic lights red, yellow, and green?

Smith, Douglas B. *Ever Wonder Why?* New York: Fawcett Gold Medal, 1992.

Zotti, Ed. *Know It All!* New York: Ballantine Books, 1993.

92. What do gold, tents, a blacksmith, and the country of France have to do with your blue jeans?

Buchman, Dian Dincin, and Seli Groves. *What If? Fifty Discoveries That Changed the World.* New York: Scholastic, 1988.

Caney, Steven. *Steven Caney's Invention Book.* New York: Workman Publishing, 1985.

Felder, Deborah H. *The Kids' World Almanac of History.* New York: Pharos Books, 1991.

Garrison, Webb. *Why Didn't I Think of That? From Alarm Clocks to Zippers.* Englewood Cliffs, N. J.: Prentice Hall, 1977.

Gray, Ralph, ed. *Small Inventions That Make a Big Difference.* Washington, D.C.: The National Geographic Society, 1984.

Harris, Harry. *Good Old-Fashioned Yankee Ingenuity.* Chelsea, Mich.: Scarborough House, 1990.

Morris, Scot. *The Emperor Who Ate the Bible and More Strange Facts and Useless Information.* New York: Doubleday, 1991.

Robertson, Patrick. *The Book of Firsts.* New York: Bramhall House, 1974.

Time-Life Books, eds. *Inventive Genius.* Alexandria, Va.: Time-Life Books.

Wallace, Amy and Irving, and David Wallechinsky. *Significa.* New York: E. P. Dutton, 1983.

93. Where did the dessert with the wiggle come from?

Campbell, Hannah. *Why Did They Name It . . . ?* New York: Ace Books, 1964.

Harris, Harry. *Good Old-Fashioned Yankee Ingenuity.* Chelsea, Mich.: Scarborough House Publishers, 1990.

Meyers, James. *Eggplants, Elevators, Etc.: An Uncommon History of Common Things.* New York: Hart Publishing Co., 1978.

94. How can making a mistake make you money?

Vare, Ethlie Ann and Greg Placek. *Women Inventors and Their Discoveries.* Minneapolis: Oliver Press, 1993.

95. Which toy was invented specifically to help students study?

Asakawa, Gil, and Leland Rucker. *The Toy Book.* New York: Alfred A. Knopf, 1992.

Gray, Ralph, ed. *Small Inventions That Make a Big Difference.* Washington, D.C.: The National Geographic Society, 1984.

Martinet, Jeanne. *The Year You Were Born: A Day-by-Day Record of 1987.* New York: Tambourine Books, 1993.

Wulffson, Don L. *Extraordinary Stories behind the Invention of Ordinary Things.* New York: Lothrop, Lee, and Shepard Books, 1981.

96. How was a whole country fooled?

Manchester, Richard B. *Incredible Facts.* New York: Galahad Books, 1985.

97. What job could you do if you couldn't hear or speak?

McWhirter, Norris and Ross. *Guinness Book of Phenomenal Happenings.* New York: Sterling Publishing Co., 1976.

98. Why did a school put a traffic light in its lunchroom?

Sobol, Donald J. *Encyclopedia Brown's Third Record Book of Weird and Wonderful Facts.* New York: William Morrow and Co., 1985.

99. What letter is used most often in the English language?

Felton, Bruce. *One of a Kind.* New York: William Morrow and Co., 1992.

Perko, Marko. *Did You Know That . . . ?* New York: Berkley Books, 1994.

Reader's Digest Facts and Fallacies. New York: The Reader's Digest Assn., 1988.

Wulffson, Don L. *Extraordinary Stories behind the Invention of Everyday Things.* New York: Lothrop, Lee, and Shepard Books, 1981.

100. Why wouldn't a locksmith give anyone his key?

Polley, Jane, ed. *Stories Behind Everyday Things.* New York: Reader's Digest Assn., 1980.

SCRIPTURE INDEX

Philippians 2:9	54	Psalm 69:7	18
Philippians 4:5	153	Psalm 71:5	76
Proverbs 3:9-10	14	Psalm 71:17	45
Proverbs 12:10	98	Psalm 93:4	109
Proverbs 16:28	111	Psalm 103:2	66
Proverbs 16:31	149	Psalm 104:14	117
Proverbs 17:22	97	Psalm 125:2	127
Proverbs 25:19	96	Psalm 135:13	27
Proverbs 27:23	28	Psalm 139:13	34
Psalm 5:12	152	Psalm 139:18	129
Psalm 17:5	118	Psalm 142:7	155
Psalm 19:12	39	Psalm 145:16	30
Psalm 24:7	116	Psalm 146:8	69
Psalm 27:10	84	Psalm 147:3	10
Psalm 30:11	83	Romans 2:7	6
Psalm 32:9	56	Revelation 3:7	172
Psalm 34:1-2	23	Revelation 22:17	48
Psalm 40:5	134